Manet

Nicholas Wadley

Manet

The Colour Library of Art
Paul Hamlyn·London

Acknowledgments

The paintings in this volume are reproduced by kind permission of the following collections, galleries and museums to which they belong: The Dowager Lady Aberconway, London (Plate 36); Art Institute of Chicago; A. A. Munger Collection (Plate 19); Art Institute of Chicago: Potter Palmer Collection (Plates 13, 31); Bibliothèque Nationale, Paris (Figures 2, 3); Bührle Collection, Zurich (Plate 41); Cincinnati Art Museum, Ohio (Plate 12); Courtauld Institute Galleries, London (Plates 8, 48); Estate of the Late Jakob Goldschmidt, New York (Plate 49); M. Knoedler & Co, New York (Figure 6); Kunsthalle, Bremen (Plate 17); Kunsthalle, Hamburg (Plate 46); Metropolitan Museum of Art, New York: Gift of Erwin Davies, 1889 (Plate 18); Metropolitan Museum of Art, New York: Bequest of Mrs H. O. Havemeyer, 1929. The H. O. Havemeyer Collection (Plates 7, 11); Metropolitan Museum of Art, New York: Gift of William Church Osborne, 1949 (Plate 3); Metropolitan Museum of Art, New York: Rogers Fund 1919 (Figure 4); Musée des Beaux-Arts, Tournai (Plates 35, 44); Musée du Louvre, Paris (Plates 9, 10, 14, 16, 20, 25, 29, 32, 39, 40, 45); Museu de Arte, São Paulo, Brazil (Plate 42); Museum of Fine Arts, Boston: Gift of W. G. R. Allen (Figure 5); Museum of Fine Arts, Boston, on anonymous loan (Plate 6); Trustees of the National Gallery, London (Plates 5, 21, 22, 38); National Gallery of Art, Washington D.C.: Chester Dale Collection (Plate 4); National Gallery of Art, Washington D.C.: Gift of Horace Havemeyer in memory of his mother Louisine W. Havemeyer (Plate 33); Neue Staatsgalerie, Munich (Plates 27, 28); Ny Carlsberg Glyptotek, Copenhagen (Plate 2); Petit Palais, Paris (Plate 24); Philadelphia Museum of Art, Pennsylvania: Mr and Mrs Carroll S. Tyson Collection (Plate 34); Rouart Collection, Paris (Plates 1, 15, 30); Shelburne Museum, Shelburne, Vermont: On loan from Electra Havemeyer Webb Fund Inc. (Plates 26, 37); Staatliche Museen, Nationalgalerie, Berlin-Dahlem (Plate 43); Stadtische Kunsthalle, Mannheim (Plate 23); Stedelijk Museum, Amsterdam; On loan from Private Collection (Plate 47). The following photographs were supplied by Joachim Blauel, Munich (Plates 27, 28); Geoffrey Clements, New York (Plates 3, 11); Walter Drayer, Zurich (Plate 41); Giraudon, Paris (Plate 20); Andre Held/Joseph P. Ziolo, Paris (Plate 40); Michael Holford, London (Plates 1, 8, 9, 10, 15, 21, 22, 24, 29, 30, 32, 36, 38, 39, 48); Ralph Kleimhempel, Zurich (Plate 46); Jules Messiaen, Tournai (Plates 35, 44); Eric Pollitzer, New York (Plate 49); Scala, Florence (Plates 14, 16, 45); Pieter Scheier, São Paulo (Plate 42); Gustav Schwarz, Mannheim (Plate 31); Hermann Stickelmann, Bremen (Plate 17); A. J. Wyatt, Philadelphia (Plate 34). The frontispiece is reproduced by courtesy of the Mansell Collection, London.

Published by Paul Hamlyn Limited
Drury House · Russell Street · London WC2
© Paul Hamlyn Ltd 1967
Printed in Italy by Officine Grafiche Arnoldo Mondadori, Verona

Contents

2 Study for 'Olympia'

Introduction

The name Edouard Manet conjures up visions of an elegantly well-bred member of the Parisian bourgeoisie, respectable to the point of affectation. It conjures up thoughts of an accomplished artist very much at odds with the taste of his day, rejected almost to a point beyond his endurance. Manet is invariably associated with those other dissentient painters, the French Impressionists: at the time of their first group exhibition in 1874 he was even spoken of as their leader. He mixed with them socially, knew them well and—like them—he painted the world around him in very direct and unpretentious terms. The impressionist scenes of Parisian life that he painted during the 1870s are generally considered as the climax of his artistic achievement, after an early period of confusion and uncertainty.

But Manet persistently refused to exhibit with the Impressionists and was once mortified to be mistakenly congratulated for two Monet seascapes. A study of his life reveals important differences of principle between Manet and the Impressionist group. A close examination of his paintings suggests that his real importance and originality as an artist also lie well outside the field of Impressionism. The initial appearance given by his life-work of a series of objective impressions of everyday reality is misleading and the popular assessment of his figure paintings of the 1870s as the fullest realisation of his potential is in fact a gross over-simplification. Not only are some of the paintings of the 1860s far more impressive to look at, but they are also far richer in new ideas and implications than anything he did later. The second half of the 1860s is undoubtedly the most significant period of his career. It was only after losing the balance he had acquired during those years between his objective vision and his inventive intuition that he resorted to a concept much closer to that of the Impressionists, and for a while even adopted their technique of painting.

Manet's place in the history of art is an uncomfortable perch astride the middle of the nineteenth century, an uncomfortable enough time for any thinking artist and for a man of Manet's temperament, an acute degree of discomfort was inevitable.

The most immediate problem for the nineteenth century artist was to reassess his position in society, a society which was still feeling the effects of the major social and industrial changes of the century's early years. The working environment of the artist was becoming more materialistic, urban-centred and bourgeois-dominated. The stable and informed patronage of the nobility (a discriminating minority) had been replaced by the status-conscious demands of the bourgeoisie (a relatively uninformed majority with unschooled taste and little real sense of tradition). One solution of the more progressive artists to this situation was to try to come to terms with society, in the belief that art should be of and about society, reflecting society's worthwhile values, and that in doing so it might even improve that society. The other extreme solution was in effect to escape from the problem, to ignore, or reject a worthless society and to withdraw into an art that was only concerned with artistic values, a pure *art-for-art's-sake*. Manet's solution was both of these things. His conscious ambition was essentially to be 'of his time', but at the same time his instincts led him towards an exclusive and revolutionary involvement with aesthetic conderations almost despite that ambition. This duality makes his life and work not just the sad story of a misunderstood individual, but a rich and unique expression of the century's peculiar character.

In order to examine these points it is most convenient to consider first the extraordinary love-hate relationship that grew up between Manet and the society he wanted to embrace and be embraced by, and afterwards to trace, through his works, his uneven evolution as a painter. The two aspects are inseparable in that the unevenness of Manet's achievement was to some extent caused by the disruptive effect of his struggle with society. Furthermore, any consideration of Manet's relationship with his times involves all the major preoccupations of the nineteenth century artist. These include the artist's self-assertion as an individual; his attitude towards tradition; his interest in the exotic and oriental; his investigation of new technical means; the ideas, advice and criticism of contemporary writers and—most important—his attitude towards society both as a patron and as the subject matter of his art.

The drastic influence of social change on the artist's world is clearly illustrated by what happened to the Salon which was the setting for Manet's public encounter with society. The Salon was Paris's most important exhibition of painting and sculpture, usually held annually, but sometimes every other year—the forerunner of the Royal Academy summer shows. Since its foundation in the mid–seventeenth century the Salon had been a small exhibition, reserved exclusively for members of the French Academy and patronised by the court and the aristocracy. During the early nineteenth century it grew into a vast public occasion, open—subject to jury—to all artists and open—subject to nothing but social and political prejudice—to the bourgeoisie as a spectacle. The succession of large galleries, their walls covered with paintings two or three deep from eye-level to ceiling, became a fashionable and diverting meeting place. This was the unestablished artist's only means of reaching prospective purchasers. The painter Ingres called it 'a bazaar in which the tremendous number of objects is overwhelming and business rules instead of art'. The most influential art criticism of the year was written during the six weeks of the Salon each Spring. The public looked to the jury and the critics for guidance and the jury and many of the critics had public taste very much in mind during their deliberations. The outcome of this vicious circle was a debased and faceless form of acceptable art, undemanding in its story-telling content and reassuringly indulgent in form.

To Manet the Salon was 'the real field of battle'. He believed in this absolutely as a matter of principle. By birth and by inclination he was a man of the Parisian near-aristocracy, elegantly fastidious in dress and manner, rather reserved and careful about his company. He showed no real desire to disown his social status—he seems to have relished playing the discreet dandy in the café society over which he and Degas reigned—and he was by nature something of a respecter of tradition and convention. Manet's feelings about the Salon were that the established structure, for all its limitations, existed, and that he was obliged to accept it and achieve recognition (which was important to him) within these limitations if at all. But this is not to say that he complied with official taste in doing so.

After the promising award of an 'Honourable Mention' for *The Guitarist* at only his second Salon in 1861, the history of Manet's Salon submissions is one of frequent rejection and the most prolonged barrage of wilful criticism and public hostility to confront any nineteenth century painter. *Le Déjeuner sur l'Herbe* in 1863 and *Olympia* in 1865 provoked the most spectacular outbursts, but these were not isolated incidents. The isolated incidents were the success of *Le Bon Bock* in 1873 and his appointment to the Légion d'Honneur in 1882 (which was in any case engineered by his friend Antonin Proust). In 1882 it was still unexceptional for a critic to write about Manet as 'a painter who has not even the elementary qualification of knowing his trade'.

The effect of this reception on Manet was slow to develop. At first there was a long period of naive incredulity. During his six years as an Ecole des Beaux Arts student he had vainly believed right up to the end that his teacher (Thomas Couture) would come round to his way of thinking. So now he felt convinced that the public hostility of the early 1860s could be only a shortlived misunderstanding. Manet had gained an early success, the admiration of younger painters and the support of the poet and critic Baudelaire. His slightly ingenuous confidence is reflected in the dandified pose and light-hearted provocativeness of these years and in a sincere note of bewildered protest in his letter to Baudelaire in 1865.

The renewed criticism of Manet's paintings in 1865 produced a change of mood and the first of several serious crises of confidence. These were interspersed by and probably urged on the sustained effort that led to his masterpieces of 1866-9: *Le Fifre, The Execution of Maximilian, Portrait of Zola, Le Déjeuner à l'Atelier, Le Balcon*. Their achievement was to be matched nowhere in the works of the 1870s when his concentration seemed diluted and the developed nature of his masterpieces was dissipated into several different manners running side by side, each one less assured.

The last important project, the *Bar aux Folies-Bergère* of 1881-2 has been hailed by some writers as the potential beginning—had Manet lived—of a new and greater phase in his oeuvre; but it seems only a shadow of his earlier large-scale compositions. The weakened resolution and lost certainty of the 1870s and the final bitterness, inflamed by his ill-health in the 1880s betray a sensitivity blunted by prolonged and deliberate abuse.

Baudelaire had recognised from the start how vulnerable Manet was. His temperament was not resilient like that of his contemporary Courbet, a painter who thrived on opposition. Manet needed recognition and leant heavily on the support of Baudelaire, Zola, Mallarmé and others. The strength of his art lay not in the aggressively self-assertive form and content of Courbet's, but in a refined and sensitive intuition: Baudelaire and Mallarmé recognised this too. Manet's later work did not lose its earlier commitment to a particular field of subject matter; nor did he lose the sharp-

ness of his eye or the facility of his touch; but the instinct that had fused these into a series of very great paintings no longer prevailed.

This suggests several questions. Should this apparent lack of stamina qualify our assessment of Manet as an artist? What great artist ever allowed circumstances—however unfavourable—to overpower his belief in himself and his art? Why didn't he just ignore them? There are two points to be made here. First, the option open to the nineteenth century artist to 'ignore' his public was a new and still-forming circumstance. The introspectiveness of 'Romantics' like Goya, Blake and Delacroix early in the century; the commanding taunting attitude adopted by Courbet in the 1850s and the gestural escape from civilisation by Gauguin at the end of the century, these are extreme examples of artists resolving their new situation. Insecurity and uncertainty were built into it. Manet was the first artist to walk the plank of bourgeois taste. He attempted to ride out the shortcomings of the official artistic structure—which, incidentally, was radically overhauled within ten years of his death. His suffering at its hands was extreme and not devoid of victimisation. Any established artist could expect at least a minor award at the Salon and thereby be free to submit what works he pleased for exhibition, by-passing the Jury. Manet was denied this privilege by comfortably established jurors until two years before his death.

The second point has already been mentioned; that his decision not to 'opt out of society' stemmed from a very deliberate and fundamental principle. Manet belonged to society and believed his art to be about society—not politically, but in a human, fashionable and richly contemporary sense. Had he not felt this so strongly, his non-acceptance by a society that other artists could dismiss as not worth bothering about, would scarcely have mattered. But since Manet did feel this way, however naive or misguided it might seem

3 Portrait of Baudelaire

to us in our wisdom, it is hardly surprising that when he died in 1883, he was embittered, disillusioned, and cynical about his late and grudging recognition. The paradox of the situation is that the driving enthusiasm behind his art (he lived, ate and slept painting and seldom spoke of anything else) prevented him from ever understanding the reasons for the criticism that disturbed him so deeply.

Manet's commitment to the world around him was not in itself exceptional. The drift of much mid-century French painting was towards 'naturalism' of one sort or another: the landscapes of Corot and the Barbizon painters, the peasant paintings of Millet and Courbet, the urban working scenes of Daumier. Nevertheless Manet's interest in this kind of subject was a bad start as far as public relations went. The suspicions that such subjects contained political implications—a suspicion in some cases justified, disturbed the bourgeoisie's feeling of security. In this respect Couture's recorded verdict on Manet as a student—'My poor boy, you will never be more than the Daumier of your day'—was doubly loaded. But, despite Manet's political beliefs, which were firmly left-wing republican, there is little political comment in his painting and little evidence of active participation in politics in his letters or conduct. Too much is made by some writers of the Daumier-like qualities of *The Absinthe Drinker* of 1858-9 (plate 2) and of two passing references to Napoleon III in adolescent letters of 1849. Any later unfavourable references that Manet made to the Emperor or his regime were primarily concerned with the artistic establishment for which Napoleon was nominally responsible.

The particular sort of 'naturalism' that preoccupied Manet had already been formulated by Baudelaire who was Manet's constant companion from about 1860-2 and close friend until the poet's death in 1867. In his *Le Peintre de la Vie Moderne* (1863) Baudelaire wrote that the modern artist's real problem lay in 'selecting what is beautiful from what is present'. As early as 1845 he had written: 'the heroism of modern life surrounds us and urges us on . . . He will be truly a painter, the painter who will know how to draw out of our daily life its epic aspect, and make us see in colour and design, how we are great and poetic in our neckties and polished boots'. This last phrase is significant in its apparent triviality. For Baudelaire, as for Manet, the 'epic aspect' of modern life was not the pathos-full *social-realism* of Millet and Daumier. *Le Peinture de la Vie Moderne* was in fact an admiring appraisal of the drawings and water-colours of Constantin Guys (1805-92) who approached Bau-delaire's ideal of the modern artist—an impersonal observer, his personality concealed, mixing in the fashionable crowd, absorbing and recording every glance, gesture and pose, every characteristic oddity of costume, pattern and colour, every-thing that comprised the essential appearance of the era. Manet came to know and admire Guys, but could never share Baudelaire's total faith in him as the complete artist.

The impersonality of Manet's art in the 1860s is one of its most remarkable features. He became so successful in looking at the world 'from the outside' that we are scarcely aware of the man, his marriage to Suzanne Leenhoff, his problems. Even the nature of the disease which killed him—discreetly referred to by all biographers as 'a serious illness'—remains elusive. His art contains no emotional autobiography: as a person he stands aloof, with dandified reserve. This quality of personal withdrawal from his art is heightened in the later 1860s by the flat, unvaried way in which he actually applied his paint to canvas, devoid of individual mannerisms.

In other ways too Manet was ready-made for the role that Baudelaire prescribed. His shrewd eye and his deft touch worked well together and he was already devoted to the contemporary world as subject matter—this issue was the cause of his arguments with Couture in the 1850s. Manet's daily contact and discussion with Baudelaire gave confidence to his early ideas. *La Musique aux Tuileries* of 1862 (plate 5) demonstrates more than any other of the early works, Manet's Baudelairean eye for the contemporary scene, on his own social level.

The Absinthe Drinker is a romantic symbol of the contempo-rary world, *The Street Singer* (plate 6) an ordinary incident from that world and *The Old Musician* (plate 4) is an extraor-dinary allegory about it. *La Musique aux Tuileries* on the other hand represents an ambitious essay into pictorial journalism. It comprises a succession of observations of the habits and appearance of real people (Manet's own social circle) in a real setting (the Tuileries gardens in Paris). It is a record of their hats and veils, their fans and parasols, their best-dressed children and the fancy chairs. The painting contains many portraits, not all known to us but obviously recognisable in their day; the unmistakable profile of Baudelaire appears beneath a tree towards the left—(see figure 3). The painting does not tell a co-ordinated story and has no real unity of composition. The interest and emphasis shift, like the light falling through the trees, from incident to incident across the canvas. It is the visual equivalent of someone moving among the crowd with a tape-recorder snatching fragments from different conversations, some clearer than others. Manet visited the Tuileries every day after lunch and the crowded mass of motifs was based on the many sketches made then. These separate fragments are only loosely held together: first by an overall balance between black and coloured areas, secondly by the great curving arcs of the tree trunks. The trunks sprout from the crowd at different points in depth, but echo one another so closely in shape and tone that they succeed in holding the space intact and in relating the sparkling crowd scene to the sombre foliage overhead. But the effect of this device is not immediately apparent; the first impression is that of lively confusion, heightened by the spontaneous, uneven technique.

La Musique was one of the first paintings to arouse criticism of Manet's 'inept' technique. Even a sympathetic critic, Theodore Duret, later wrote of Manet that 'he began to paint before knowing enough about handling a brush . . . Even as a beginner, when he understood his craft very imperfectly, he began to paint spontaneously, relying on his own inspiration without preoccupying himself with principles and procedures familiar to the studios . . . ' Certainly *La Musique* gives a feeling of the artist's exuberant enthusiasm carrying him along with no apparent thought of composition, perspective or finish. More than one biographer of Manet has taken up this point and discussed his early work in terms of a 'faulty sense of design', 'fallible sense of scale' and inability to cope with perspective or anatomy. The strung-out, piecemeal composition of *The Old Musician* has been cited as an example and so has the spatial ambiguity of *Mlle Victorine in the Costume of an Espada* (plate 7) of which J. Richardson in his book *Manet* (London 1958) has said: 'his sense of scale has let him down so badly that the bull-fighting scene makes an annoying hole in the decorative schema and points up the unreality of this costume-piece instead of giving it the air of authenticity which it so sorely needs.'

When considering whether or not these characteristics resulted from a lack of ability, it is necessary to look ahead to the development of Manet's painting after 1863, which suggests that he was consciously unconcerned with the conventions of pictorial illusionism (that is, using perspective and a subtle range of tonal modelling to create the illusion of reality) and that he was very obviously interested in the formal arrangement of his paintings. The seeming artlessness of *La Musique*'s composition and execution was no accident. As in the two racecourse paintings *Women at the Races* (plate 12) and *Races at Longchamp* (plate 13) of 1864, it contributes enormously to the evocation of a moment. This *is* a sort of illusionism, the instant illusionism of Impressionist painting.

The painting of Mlle Victorine, on the other hand, never set out to attain that sort of truth. The artist openly admits in the title that this is a costume-piece, a charade: his model is dressed up to play a part. The pictorial means are no less openly artificial; Manet does not pretend that the space behind the model's stark silhouette is a 'real' (that is, completely illusionistic) space. The motif of the bullfight is almost an emblem—as if painted on a backcloth—related to the main figure not in scale but in theme. The division between the two is marked by the otherwise arbitrary tone-change half way up the background. At the same time a formal relationship between them is maintained by the coincident diagonal of the picador's lance and Victorine's sword.

It would be more relevant to compare Manet's treatment of the subject here to the symbolic artifice of late medieval altarpieces than to the rationalised illusionism of post-Renaissance paintings. In these altarpieces the large figure of the saint is usually isolated against a gold ground and flanked by compositions of tiny figures representing various significant incidents from the saint's life: they too are related in subject to the main figure, but not in scale or, necessarily, technique.

The bull-fighting incident in *Mlle Victorine in the Costume of an Espada* is like a pictorial inscription that serves to identify the subject.

Once we accept that such an approach to composition exists in this painting—however intuitively at this stage—it is possible to recognise traces of it in other early works. The only significant difference between this painting and *The Guitarist* (plate 3), wich is also a posed costume-piece, is that in the latter the 'backcloth' is not painted, but is just a dark foil to the simple, strongly contrasted tones of the figure. In both of these paintings (and in the *Portrait of the Artist's Parents* (plate 1), *The Absinthe Drinker*, also *The Old Musician*) the motif is pushed right forward towards the picture surface on a very shallow stage; any recession behind the motif is either disguised in half-statement or even openly denied.

How can this contrived artificiality of composition be reconciled with Manet's ambition to be a painter of modern life with all its casual movement? Simply by realising that he was in the process of discovering that the naturalism of *La Musique* with its anticipation of Impressionist techniques was not necessarily the best way of achieving his ambition. Neither was it the approach that he used throughout the 1860s. What is perhaps more significant is that for all his dismissal of orthodox studio techniques, Manet was an artist conscious of tradition.

The technical originality of Manet's early work was not in itself unrelated to his intensive study and copying of traditional art in the Louvre and in museums abroad. The brilliant frontal lighting of *The Guitarist*, dramatically simplifying the tonal contrasts, is reminiscent of Caravaggio, and of his influence on seventeenth century Spanish painting which always took pride of place in Manet's taste for the past. *The Absinthe Drinker*, Manet said, 'was executed with the technical simplicity I had discovered in Velasquez.' Although there were few paintings by the Spanish artist in Paris and Manet's real discovery of him was still to come, the inspiration of Velasquez is richly apparent in Manet's early work with its fluid use of paint, simple tones and cool colour. The frieze-like composition and strange, airless space of *The Old Musician* is directly related to the Velasquez painting *Los Borrachos* of which Manet owned a print.

Clearly Manet's ambition was not to disown traditional art. He felt free to reconcile it in a very personal way with his own interests and instincts. Just as in *The Old Musician* he had quoted from one of his own paintings (plate 2), so he felt free to quote at will from the paintings of the past. In the two major works of 1863—*Le Déjeuner sur l'Herbe* (plate 9) and *Olympia* (plate 14)—Manet borrows freely

from Giorgione, Raphael and Titian. This must have been a deliberate trial of strength. In these two paintings more obviously than in any others, Manet was seeking to marry the tradition he respected but thought abused with the contemporary spirit that could give it fresh meaning.

This sounds as if the paintings were the result of a carefully pre-conceived programme; by Manet's later standards they were. The idea for *Le Déjeuner sur L'Herbe* came, so Antonin Proust tells us, while they were walking together along the banks of the Seine past some people bathing in the sunlight. Manet recalled Giorgione's idyllic pastorale, *La Fête Champêtre*, which they had copied as students in the Louvre, saying, 'It's black that painting . . . I should like to do the subject over again in terms of the transparency of atmospheric light, with people like those bathers over there.' This could (almost) be an Impressionist talking, but Manet's procedure was not to take his easel to the spot. Instead he brought models into his studio and set them in a pose borrowed directly from Raphael (see figure 4). What could be more self-consciously contrived? There is even a playful wit about his modernisation of the Raphael motif: the substitution of a cane for a River God's reeds and the introduction of the bird (scarcely visible, hovering against the foliage while prospecting for a perch) to 'explain' the otherwise empty gesture in this new context of the right hand figure's outstretched finger.

Manet always worked from a model and usually went to great pains to get an authentic model. He tried hard to find a real street entertainer to pose for *The Street Singer* and he *did* find a cadet for *Le Fifre*, a waitress for *La Servante de Bocks*, soldiers for *The Execution of Maximilian*, a famous courtesan for *Nana* and a barmaid for the *Bar aux Folies-Bergère*. He always took them back to his studio, often contriving an appropriate background for them with stage properties. This is clearly at variance with any proto-Impressionist

4 Engraving after Raphael's 'Judgement of Paris' (detail)

naturalism and is reminiscent of the academic stickling for authenticity found in Napoleonic battle pictures.

There is apparent conflict in *Le Déjeuner sur l'herbe* between the 'outdoor realism' of the landscape and the 'studio realism' of the figures and still life—contradictions of lighting, scale, detail, etc. The painting as we see it, offers little evidence that while Manet was actually working on the canvas his original intention to paint a freshly-naturalistic, outdoor scene was still foremost in his mind. What we can see is evidence of a further development of his technique. As in *The Guitarist*, the tonality of the main figures suggests that there is a brilliant frontal light source which has the effect of reducing their volume; at the same time the hard contours emphasise the suggestion of cut-out silhouettes. In the seated nude there is virtually no modulation of colour or tone from one contour to the other. Down the line of her back there is no softening of tone (the academic convention for suggesting that the form continues beyond our vision) but a sudden contrast. The actual technique of painting such a passage was also thoroughly unconventional: instead of working up from thinly-painted dark tones to the more 'meaty' paint of the highlights as was orthodox studio practice, the light tones were flatly painted right across the form to start with and the few marks of shadow were then drawn in on top. The cool colour range in *Le Déjeuner* is related throughout the painting. The dark areas (such as the hair of the distant figure) are boldly emphasised regardless of their position apart in space.

All of these things show Manet experimenting with the mechanics of a painting at the expense of conventional means, at the expense of illusionistic representation, and—what is more significant—in a way that contributes nothing to our understanding of the subject matter. It is as if the act of painting was becoming a separate activity from the preconception of the subject matter. Once he had satisfied the conceptual side of the painting in arranging his motif, he seems almost to have relinquished his interest in it.

Emile Zola, a frequent visitor to Manet's studio, must have watched and talked to Manet while he was working. He wrote of Manet's 'departure for the unknown with each white canvas he placed on the easel'. He criticised the opportunism of Manet's method but commended the sharpness and honesty of his eye. By honesty he meant two things. First, that Manet's perception of the subject in front of him was unprejudiced: he looked at the colours, tones and shapes that were actually there rather than perceiving them intellectually as parts of a body, a coat, a still life and so on. (Manet himself once said 'nature never gives you anything but references'.) A second kind of perceptiveness was present in the development of relationships between these colours, tones and shapes on the canvas. In this second stage the eye was looking as much at the painting as at the original subject. It was on his intuitive and improvisatory balance of colour and tone relationships that the evolving 'unknown' nature of each painting depended. During the actual execution, any 'literary' meaning (any story-telling or symbolic aspects of the subject matter) was abandoned to the free play of his inventive instincts and the facility of his brush. In *Le Déjeuner* the blandly impersonal treatment of the nude, however invitingly her smile looks out towards us, denies any element of seduction. The sensuality of the figure is the sensuality of paint, not of woman. The suggestions of impropriety by public and critics probably reflected their sense of shock in face of such an unorthodox technique as much as any genuine sensations of moral affront. D. S. MacColl once said words to the effect that the public, faced with any innovation in art, experienced the sensations of indecent assault. Such was Manet's crime against society.

The same qualities are all present in *Olympia* (plate 14). This too was based on a Renaissance prototype—Titian this time—which Manet had copied as a student (plate 15). The borrowing is even more pointed than in *Le Déjeuner sur l'Herbe* with very detailed references in motif and composition. The intention to revise a hallowed iconography from the past in a modern idiom is unmistakable.

Even clearer is the rapid maturing of Manet's idiom. His dispassionately objective observation of the motif is transcribed with a remarkable economy of means. Because this is an interior and not a landscape, there is no diffusion of light through foliage and so on; Manet could impose an absolute control on the space and colour of the painting. The background is a simple dark screen, absorbing the servant's head and the cat; the rest falls into a single high-toned area. The ruthless improvisation of his borrowed motif—Zola spoke of his 'tender brutality'—is almost as simple as that. Half-

tones are virtually eliminated and variations of colour within each tonal mass are exquisitely refined: it is the play between these that creates a sense of plastic relief in the painting.

Manet's interest in the technique of Japanese prints must have contributed to this new assurance. Even his drawing has a new strength. The slight, highly selective inflections of the contour and a few touches of smoky shadow enabled him to paint whole areas of *Olympia's* body in unmodulated colour without denying it substance. The painting is a masterpiece and bearing its subject matter in mind, it is also undeniably an heroic milestone of mid-century naturalism, despite the fact that it was thoroughly conceptual in its origins and thoroughly un-naturalist in its total effect. *Olympia* is an epic symbol of contemporary life, the traditional 'homage to Venus' apparatus accorded to an objective statement of reality.

Olympia herself (recognisably posed by the model of *Le Déjeuner*) is unidealised and again unsensual, despite her unabashed stare and despite the casual intimacy of her cast-off slipper, her ribbon and the black velvet neckband—still a seduction symbol in popular art and fiction. Certain writers from Manet's time onwards have recognised in her a disturbing hypnotic aloofness that echoes Baudelaire's concept of woman. G. H. Hamilton (see the book list on page 22) quotes from several poems in *Les Fleurs du Mal* which contain certain parallels to the iconography of *Olympia*. One passage is roughly translatable as follows:

Her eyes fixed on me like a caged tiger, she goes through a series of poses that are dream-like and mysterious. The fusion of candour and wantonness lends a new charm to each transition. Her arms and her leg and her thigh and her loins, glistening as if polished with oil, undulating like a swan, pass before my blissful, all-seeing eyes; and her stomach and her breasts, the grapes of my vine...

and another:

'Where there is nothing but gold, steel, light and gems, burning for ever like a useless star, the cold majesty of the sterile woman.'

Zola felt obliged to deny strenuously any connection between Manet's painting and Baudelaire's poetry (the relevant article is quoted on pages 28, 29) and in terms of this sort of coincidence of imagery he seems justified. The powerful impact of *Olympia* is no more 'the cold majesty of sterile woman' than it is the glowing majesty of Titian's fertile *Urbino Venus*. The imaginative poetry of Manet's painting stems from its exotic colour harmonies, its strange tonality and the charm of his touch. In these lies the true equivalent to Baudelaire's sensuous and sometimes macabre expressiveness and there are remarkable similarities to be found in the actual range of colour evoked by Baudelaire. It is these qualities that make *Olympia* an image of romantic mystery and ambiguity and these are what appealed to Mallarmé who spoke of the 'exquisite nuances' of Manet's use of black.

The same qualities are all richly present in *Le Déjeuner à l'Atelier* (plate 27), a subject which in itself is so banal so as to allow no Baudelairean romanticising, unless one is prepared to make much of the presence of another of Manet's cats, licked in with a few deft strokes of velvet black. The enthusiasm that Manet and Baudelaire shared for cats is another thought-provoking coincidence, but Manet's breed have little of the mystery of the cats in Baudelaire's poems. In that marvellous aside in his letter to Manet (see page 28) Baudelaire asks about the contents of the painting 'is it *really* a cat?' with a mixture of delight and disbelief.

Manet showed often enough, in his deliberate and unashamed borrowing from other artists, and in his insistence upon working from a model, that he had little interest in the original invention of motifs. He certainly had little literary imagination and later complained to Mallarmé that he found it impossible to follow the wandering fantasies of 'you terrible poets'. It was the same trait in his temperament that led him to say of the symbolist painter Gustave Moreau, 'I have a lively sympathy for him, but he takes us back to the in-

comprehensible, while we wish that everything be understood.'

Understanding was the last thing these paintings achieved with the public and critics. In this respect Manet's association with Baudelaire cannot have helped: Baudelaire had been brought to trial after the publication of *Les Fleurs du Mal* in 1857 and six of the poems had been suppressed as indecent. Possibly Baudelaire's public championship of Manet contributed to the accusations of indecency levelled against both *Le Déjeuner sur l'Herbe* and *Olympia* (some are quoted on pages 26, 27). Manet was also accused of an eclectic dependence on Velasquez, Goya and El Greco and, as one might expect, critics were outraged by his uninhibited borrowing from the revered art of the Italian Renaissance.

The more serious criticisms—which acknowledged his talent—were of his concentration on the technique of painting at the expense of subject matter and of his deliberately abandoning paintings when they were no more than accomplished sketches. These were very perceptive appraisals of the revolutionary elements in Manet's art. Gautier for example, recognised (with dismay of course) that Manet had 'broken loose from rules accepted by centuries of logic'.

It was at this point that Manet temporarily lost faith. The confidence—possibly naiveté—that had led him to submit *Olympia* to the 1865 Salon, though he must have realised that it could only provoke the same sort of criticism as *Le Déjeuner sur l'Herbe*, now left him. After appealing to Baudelaire for sympathy (see page 28) and being firmly admonished, Manet left Paris.

Happily his escape took the form of two weeks in Spain. He visited several cities and in Madrid, at the Prado, Manet was for the first time confronted with a large number of paintings by Velasquez, his life-long idol. Goya he found disappointing, but in Velasquez he discovered what seemed to be a vote of confidence in his developing ideas. The brevity of his stay is accountable partly by the fact that he could not bear to be away from Paris and also because he wanted to start work again.

Two pictures painted on his return to Paris—*The Philosopher* (plate 19) and *Le Fifre* (plate 20)—are almost acts of homage to his master. In each case the single figure is set against a space even more airless than the intangible backgrounds he had marvelled at in Velasquez's portraits. In *Le Fifre* the spatial ambiguity of his earlier figure paintings is confidently resolved by the dense blanket of grey behind the silhouette. Line acts more as a division between flat areas of colour than as a contour around forms. Only one touch of shadow by the boy's left foot suggests a three-dimensional spatial relationship. The artist's signature, obviously written on the flat surface and deliberately placed parallel to the shadow, epitomises the painting's strange compromise between two and three dimensions. This is a more mature resolution of the problem confronted in *Mlle Victorine in Costume of an Espada*: the problem of freely combining some of the conventions of illusionistic painting with other means which unashamedly acknowledge that a painting is a flat surface with certain colours and marks made on it.

Again it is important to recognise the similarity of this technique to the simple economy of Japanese prints with their broad bands of colour, strong blacks and assured design. Manet shared the enthusiasm of his contemporaries (notably Degas and Whistler), for a tradition so refreshingly different from that revered by the academies. The contribution it made to Manet's style is an important feature of the long and complex history of oriental influence on European art of the last hundred years. In the portrait of one of the outstanding naturalist writers of his day (Zola), Manet juxtaposes a Japanese screen and print, a Velasquez composition and his own *Olympia*, thereby making a symbolic compendium of the formative ingredients of his art (plate 25).

5 Le Rendez-vous des Chats

Gautier wrote in 1868: '...when in a painting there is neither composition, nor drama, nor poetry, the technique must be perfect. And here this is not the case.' Apart from the obvious blindness to Manet's compositional sense, the main objection to this is that Manet's technique reached its peak of perfection in that very year.

Le Déjeuner à l'Atelier (plate 27) occupies a very important place in this climax. We should, perhaps, follow the title's suggestion that this is a pendant to the *Déjeuner sur l'Herbe* and in this context be fully aware of the unpretentiousness of the subject. The figures are not quoted from any Renaissance masterpiece, but are casually and rather meaninglessly posed together in the same environment. We can sympathise with Gautier's complaint that Manet's painting had no subject matter, for here there is no pretence of a narrative relationship between the figures, no heroic drama, no symbol, no allegory. It is in effect subjectless. What makes it one of the outstanding achievements of Manet's oeuvre is that it contains all Manet's qualities as a painter at their best—assurance of execution, flawless sense of interval and refinement of colour harmony. To quote Baudelaire yet again: 'great colourists know how to get an effect of colour with a black suit, a white neckcloth and a grey background.'

In *Le Déjeuner à l'Atelier* Manet achieves an extraordinary richness working within limits almost as severe as those described by Baudelaire. The harmony ranges only between the velvet black of a jacket and the silver grey of a tablecloth. The treatment of space is again a free compromise between a three-dimensional illusion and a two-dimensional arrangement. The intervals are as much on the surface as in depth. For example the colour and tone of the potted plant's leaves bring it forward to the front plane, by-passing the servant who literally stands between them. Manet almost certainly had the motif in front of him when he made such 'distortions', but they are only untruths in terms of the patently artificial

means of pictorial illusionism (making a flat surface look like what it isn't). He was true to his sensations in front of the motif and he was true to his instincts of colour and value while he was painting. These are the real 'subject matter' of Manet's painting.

Matisse describes the same attitude to painting in his *Notes of a Painter* (1908)—that of the artist who looks at each part of his motif in turn and finds a satisfactory equivalent in paint, but who must then constantly adjust the new relationship of these equivalents to each other until he arrives at a total harmony. Degas once made a vague and probably cynical reference to Manet's use of a black mirror 'to gauge values'. The importance which Manet placed upon a total harmony of values suggests that such a device may well have appealed to him. We can only wish that Manet himself had said something about it.

In the other key work of 1868-9, *Le Balcon* (plate 29), the limited colour scale is dominated by a controlled viridian. The tense passages each side of the painting, where the strong green of the railings passes across the same colour more subdued on the shutters, must be seen in the original to be fully appreciated. The electric fusion of these two planes compresses the space occupied by the figures into a flat screen once more.

Le Déjeuner à l'Atelier and *Le Balcon* are masterpieces in composition by colour. If the preceding analysis of them has been exclusively preoccupied with timeless aesthetic considerations, it is also true that through these aesthetic means Manet realised the spirit and appearance of his times. He showed '*in colour and design*, how we are great and poetic...'

The one important work of this period not so far mentioned —*The Execution of Maximilian* (plates 21, 22, 23) of which Manet made four paintings and one lithograph—was directly related to the contemporary world. This is the only significant exception to any denial of political comment in his art and his most ambitious attempt at contemporary history painting. The execution of the Emperor of Mexico in June 1867 stirred up considerable feeling in Paris, partly because Maximilian was a European, but principally because his demise was largely attributable to the calculated political manoeuvring of the French Emperor, Napoleon III. Manet worked on the project with a furious activity and on an unusually large scale. That it was particularly important to him is demonstrated by the fact that he abandoned two very large versions (the second being the mutilated National Gallery picture, plates 21 and 22) before he was satisfied. He went out of his way to incorporate authentic information from the many press reports and photographs in Parisian newspapers. Such changes as did occur between the versions (for example the imaginary landscape background of plate 21 giving way to the courtyard setting of plate 23) are directly attributable to new information becoming available.

An element of political comment was certainly recognised in Manet's composition at the time and publication of the lithograph version of the subject was prohibited by the government. A note, clearly intended for publication, which Manet sent to Duret, offers the only real insight into Manet's own feelings. It reads: 'We understand that M. Manet has been refused permission to publish a lithograph he has just made representing the execution of Maximilian. We are astonished at this action of the authorities which imposes sanctions on a work of purely artistic value.' Despite his obvious involvement in authentic modern history-painting, when it came to consideration of the finished work—whether painting or print—Manet saw its real value as 'purely artistic'. To see the final painting, as have some writers, as a dispassionate still-life painting, is to ignore the way in which Manet had collected his material and the nature of that material. But this is in effect what Manet is asking us to do.

In the Maximilian paintings the dilemma of Manet's art is most clearly posed. Here more than anywhere we are faced with the conflict between Manet's self-conscious striving towards literary modernity of subject matter and his intuitive improvisations with colour and design as self-sufficient justifications of the work of art. Here the two seem incompatible.

Manet wrote in August 1868 that as far as *grands tableaux* were concerned he had met with 'enough utter failure in things like that' to go on thinking about them. By *grands tableaux* he meant not only very big paintings, but also heroic subjects. He never attempted such subjects again with any conviction and the painting that immediately followed this series was *Le Déjeuner à l'Atelier*. The 'purely artistic' treatment of unobtrusive subject matter in that painting is clear enough and its similarity to the Maximilian paintings (in the broad flat areas of tone and harmonic colour) cannot be ignored. What these similarities make clear is that whatever his intention, when the moment of artistic realisation arrived he could, in his own words, 'never do anything but paint' and his political sympathies were insignificant, perhaps even inhibiting.

With the works of 1867-9 the homogeneous character of Manet's evolving style, which existed despite this conflict, came to an end.

The 1870s began with the disturbed months of the Prussian seige of Paris closely followed by the street-fighting which led to the downfall of the Commune. For Manet it was a decade of mixed fortune and experience, ending with the sudden first symptoms of the serious illness that was to cause his early death in 1883. He saw his young friends the Impressionists abandon the Salon (against his advice) and hold their own exhibitions. The Impressionists did not hold Manet's feelings about the role of the Salon as 'the real field of battle', —an opportunity to meet the 'opposition' on its own ground. After sharing Manet's experience of rejection and contempt, they came to see that battleground as worthless and for Pissarro at least it became a matter of principle *not* to exhibit at the Salon. Manet's own experience in the 1870s was to see his paintings rejected at four of the nine Salons. In 1871 he sold 22 paintings to the dealer Durand-Ruel, but in 1873 he was writing to a friend to borrow money. In 1873 *Le Bon Bock* achieved popular success, but in 1878 it was among several of his paintings to fetch disastrously low bids at two public auctions. He fought a grotesquely amateurish duel with a critic after a café argument in 1870 and in 1879 he coolly proposed to the Prefecture of the Seine that he should paint murals in the Hôtel de Ville. The character of his paintings during the decade was almost as various.

The most marked change in his painting was his abandonment under the influence of Impressionism of his mature 'synthetic' style, with its closed forms, flat tones and restricted palette. In the landscapes painted at Argenteuil, where he stayed with Monet and Renoir in 1874 Manet renounced his flat tones for a brilliant, flickering Impressionist display of brushwork and broken colour. Compare the heightened colour and atmospheric depth of *Argenteuil* (plate 35) with *Clair de Lune au Port de Boulogne* (plate 32) for the extent of the change in his treatment of landscapes.

The Impressionist painter of the landscape sat in front of his subject and the method he used to paint it was geared almost exclusively to evoking the impression of a moment of vision, as immediately as possible. Claude Monet for example achieved in his paintings a remarkably true evocation of the light, colour, atmosphere (and sometimes the movement) of a particular scene at a particular moment in time. Manet's Boulogne painting was not conceived as an impressionist search for open air actuality: the impression it gives is not the arresting impact of a moment, but that of a refined harmony of blacks, blues, ochre and white. In his

1874 paintings of Argenteuil and Venice (plates 35, 36 and 37) that serene timelessness has disappeared.

As this suggests, the total revision of Manet's technique was accompanied by—if not caused by—a shift of emphasis in his motivation. This constituted a revival of an almost programmatic interest in contemporary subjects for their own sake, a renewal of the belief of his student days that the painter's duty was to 'accept our times and paint what we see'. It is true that his ostensible subject matter had remained unchanged over the years; but in the 1870s Manet displayed a renewed and more conscious interest in his subjects, and in achieving visual authenticity. In the event, it proved to be at the expense of the sense of harmonic values he had developed to such a high degree in the preceding decade.

Two principal features distinguish Manet's painting of contemporary subjects from that of the Impressionists. First, he laid greater emphasis on the role of the figure in his compositions. Of the true impressionists only Renoir really shared this interest. All of the significant paintings of the 1870s—*Le Bon Bock* (plate 34), *Nana* (plate 46), *La Servante de Bocks* (plate 38), *In the Conservatory* (plate 43) and *Chez le Père Lathuile* (plate 44)—feature one or two large scale figures in the foreground.

The second important difference is related to this and illustrates another facet of Manet's changed attitude to subject matter. This is that the conception of these figures is usually not purely visual, not solely in terms of light and colour. *In the Conservatory* and *Chez le Père Lathuile* are anecdotal paintings with a strong narrative relationship between the figures; *Nana* clearly tells a story and the characterisation of the drinker in *Le Bon Bock* is richly picturesque (doubtless the reason for its popular reception). They are poised somewhere between genre portraiture and narrative painting. What lifts the best of them above the anecdotal art of contemporary academicians is the accurate perception of light values and the assured economy of their execution.

But for all their authority and contemporary spirit, these paintings no longer have the full strength of Manet's conviction behind them. They contain concessions to public taste and employ a borrowed avant-garde idiom to which Manet sacrificed a large part of his artistic personality. Degas was not wholly unjustified when he accused Manet of imitating him: the café-concert motifs with snapshot compositions that appeared among Manet's pastels and paintings of the '70s owed much to Degas.

A separate part of Manet's chronicling of his times in the 1870s was a series of portraits. They are of friends and leading figures of the day (plates 39, 40). None of them is a major work comparable with the portrait of Zola and only the superb portrait of Berthe Morisot (plate 30) displays Manet's earlier mastery. In the last five or six years of his life he also painted and drew an increasing number of lightweight fashionable portraits of society ladies (plate 45). They have an easy fluency of touch, an occasional sharp originality of colour and a soft charm that recalls Renoir's female portraits of the same period.

Manet also painted a few landscapes, seascapes and still lifes, and made one or two dispirited attempts at epic contemporary subjects. There are as well a few strangely tough works that resemble no others and are full of struggle. They include some pastel drawings of the female nude that achieve a Degas-like, sympathetic inelegance, and a few undated paintings of the same kind of subject. In *La Sultane* (plate 41) and the *Bathers* (plate 42) he tackles earlier motifs with an uncompromising breadth of handling and achieves a clumsy monumentality. They are unusual in his oeuvre and difficult to date—isolated and very personal experiments in a period of considerable uncertainty. They contain a stronger suggestion of unrealised potential than any of the better known works of the time.

The ambitions of his later years all went unrealised, including his projected series of murals of epic Parisian subjects and the crucifixion which he once revealed an ambition to paint. On the evidence of his work, this last idea seems naively out of character and offers a further suggestion of a lack of convinced direction. Ambitions still existed but he was far from confident about realising them. In the 1870s he in effect lowered his sights.

His last important statement was in fact the *Bar aux Folies-Bergère* (plate 48), another contemporary subject which suggests that his series of murals might have resembled the works of 1867-9 as much as anything of the 1870s; but perhaps this is just wishful thinking. The narrative element is suppressed and the composition achieves a certain grandeur through the simplicity of its conception and execution. The figure's frontal pose, the device of showing her distorted reflection in the mirror, and the strong horizontal emphases, all contribute to a deliberate compromise between illusionistic space and surface arrangement.

The champions of Manet's later work see the figure subjects of 1871-82 as his enduring contribution to modern art. They can compare *Nana* favourably with *Olympia* for its uncontrived modernity and see *Chez le Père Lathuile* as a remarkable advance when compared with such subjects of the late 1860s as *The Balcony* and the *Déjeuner à l'Atelier* with their theatrical properties and contrived compositions. This follows the view of Manet's contemporaries who saw him as the figure-painter of Impressionism and his enduring contribution as the accurate perception and spontaneous recording of the given moment. A favourable critic of 1880 wrote that 'one always knows when looking at his paintings just where, when, on what day, at what hour, they were painted'. Any such verdicts—including that advanced here—necessarily involve subjective value-judgements. But considering the nature of modern art, it is difficult to see what enduring contribution lies in this side of Impressionist naturalism. This was precisely the aspect of Impressionism that was climactic and retrospective rather than forward-looking.

George Moore put his finger on Manet's dilemma when he said that 'in Manet there is nothing but good painting, and there is nothing the nineteenth century dislikes as much as good painting'. Even to those critics who acknowledged his talent, Manet was only half a painter; they felt that his instinctive ability to handle paint and colour should have been harnessed to something more meaningful. What those critics had recognised—without being able to accept it—was the idea of an art in which the subject matter did not play the dominant role. An art also in which all the studio accomplishments of perspective, chiaroscuro and anatomy—those artificial contrivances that had long deceived the spectator into believing illusions—were abandoned.

What makes Manet's art meaningful now is that, for part of his career at least, he managed to prevent considerations of subject and illusion from getting in the way of his instinctive ability. It is the paintings of the 60s that look ahead to the *renaissance du sentiment classique* of Post Impressionism. In these he allowed the visual effect of the colours, shapes and tones to make its own impact on the spectator's perception. It is this patently un-artificial idea of painting that looks ahead to the wholly non-figurative art of the early twentieth century.

The pursuit of his ideas to such a conclusion in the mid-nineteenth century would of course have been unthinkable, particularly so to Manet since it would have seemed to involve the sacrifice of his ambitions for an art about society. But whether he completely realised it or not, between 1863 and 1869 Manet was demonstrating for the first time both the possibility of a subjectless art of pure sensation and that such an art can still be a very real expression of the times in which the artist lives.

BOOK LIST

The following books offer the best value in information and ideas for a more detailed study of Manet and his times.

SLOANE, Joseph C.: *French Painting between the Past and the Present 1848-1870* (Princeton, 1951)

HAMILTON, George Heard: *Manet and his Critics* (Yale, 1954)

SANDBLAD, Nils Gösta: *Manet, Three Studies in Artistic Conception* (Lund, 1954)

REWALD, John: *The History of Impressionism* (New York, 1962) (Rewald includes a good critical bibliography)

List of Salon submissions

This is a complete list of the paintings Manet submitted to the Salon. Other exhibitions and outstanding biographical items are included.

1832   Born in Paris, January 29th.

1850-56   Ecole des Beaux Arts; studio of Thomas Couture (1815-79).

1856   Travelled in Holland, Belgium, Germany and Italy.

1859   *The Absinthe Drinker* (1858-9, plate 2) rejected by the Salon jury. Met Baudelaire and Degas.

1861   *Portrait of his Parents* (1859, plate 1) and *The Guitarist* (1860, plate 3) accepted at the Salon. Latter awarded an honourable mention. Met Whistler.

1863   One man exhibition at Martinet's Gallery (14 paintings). *Mlle Victorine in the Costume of an Espada* (1862-3, plate 7), *Young Man in the Costume of a Majo* (1862-3) and *Le Déjeuner sur l'Herbe* (1862-3, plates 9 and 10) rejected at the Salon and shown at the 'Salon des Refusés'. Married Suzanne Leenhoff in Holland.

1864   *The Dead Christ* (1864, plate 11) and *Incident in the Bullring* (1863-4) a cepted at the Salon.

1865   One man exhibition at Martinet's gallery. *Olympia* (1863, plates 14 and 16), and *Christ Scourged* (1864-5) accepted at the Salon. Visit to Spain. Met Duret in Madrid.

1866   Met Zola. *The Tragic Actor* (1866) and *Le Fifre* (1865-6, plate 20) rejected at the Salon.

1867   His entry rejected at the International Exhibition in Paris. Organised independent one man show in the Place de l'Alma (50 paintings).

1868   *Portrait of Zola* (1868, plate 25) and *La Femme au Perroquet* (1866, plate 18) accepted at the Salon. Visit to London. Planned to exhibit there.

1869   *Le Balcon* (1868-9, plate 29) and *Le Déjeuner à l'Atelier* (1868, plate 27) accepted at the Salon.

1870   *The Music Lesson* (1870) and *Portrait of Eva Gonzales* (1869-70) accepted at the Salon. Franco-Prussian war. Enlisted in the National Guard.

1871   Elected to the Federation of Artists organised by the Commune (No Salon). Durand-Ruel bought 22 paintings for a total of 35,000 fr. Manet made a valued inventory of all the paintings in his studio.

1872   *The Combat between the Kearsage and the Alabama* (1864) accepted at the Salon. Visit to Holland.

1873   *Le Repos* (1869-70) and *Le Bon Bock* (1872-3, plate 34) accepted at the Salon.

1874   *Swallows* (1873) and *The Opera Ball* (1873) rejected, *The Railway* (1873, plate 33) and *Punchinelle* (1873) accepted at the Salon. First Impressionist Exhibition. Met Mallarmé. Visit to Argenteuil. Visit to Venice.

1875   *Argenteuil* (1874, plate 35) accepted at the Salon.

1876   *The Laundress* (1874) and *Portrait of Desboutin* (1875) rejected at the Salon.

1877   *Portrait of Faure as Hamlet* (1877) accepted at the Salon, *Nana* (1877, plate 46) rejected.

1878   His paintings fetched low bids at the auctions of the Faure and Hoshcedé collections. Ignored by the jury of the International Exhibition in Paris.

1879   *Boating* (1874) and *In the Conservatory* (1878-9, plate 43) accepted at the Salon.

1880   One man exhibition at La Vie Moderne (10 paintings, 15 pastels) Portrait of *Antonin Proust* (1880), and *Chez le Père Lathuile* (1879, plate 44) accepted at the Salon.

1881   *Portrait of Rochefort* (1881) and *The Lion Hunter* (1881) accepted at Salon. Awarded 2nd class medal by majority of one. (This made him *hors concours*).

1882   *Jeanne* (Spring) (1881) and *Bar aux Folies-Bergère* (1881-2, plate 48) sent to the Salon. Official appointment to the Légion d'Honneur.

1883   Underwent operation for amputation of his gangrenous left leg. Died on April 30th.
Pall-bearers were Zola, Duret, Burty, Stevens, Fantin-Latour, Monet and Proust.

1884   Memorial exhibition, Ecole des Beaux Arts (116 paintings, 7 watercolours, 26 prints, 13 drawings). Catalogue introduction by Zola.
First monograph published.
Sale of paintings in studio at death realised net total of 76,907 fr.; *Olympia* and others withdrawn.

1889   14 paintings included in International Exhibition, Paris.

1905   Special Manet section (26 paintings) at Salon d'Automne, Paris.

1932   Centenary Exhibition, Orangerie, Paris. (99 paintings and pastels, 31 watercolours and drawings).

Quotations from Manet and his contemporaries

MANET ON ART, ARTISTS AND OTHER THINGS

Couture's Studio I don't know why I'm here. Everything we see around us is ridiculous. The light is false. The shadows are false. When I come to the studio, it seems as if I am entering a tomb.

> Quoted by Antonin Proust, *Souvenirs* Paris 1913

Can't you be natural? Is that the way you stand when you go to buy a box of radishes at your grocers?

> To a model, quoted by Proust

Degas When Degas was painting Semiramis I was painting modern Paris.

> Quoted by George Moore, *Modern Painting* 1893

Velasquez What has ravished me most about Spain, what by itself has made the whole trip worthwhile is the work of Velasquez . . . the sight of his masterpieces has filled me with hope and confidence . . .
Here is the painter of painters . . . I find in him the realisation of my ideal in painting.
The background (of his portrait of Pablillos) is intangible, it is like an atmosphere that surrounds the figure who is alive and dressed completely in black.

> Letters from Spain, August 1865

Railways One day coming back from Versailles, I travelled on the footplate with the driver and fireman. What a magnificent spectacle these two men were, what sang-froid, what guts! It's a dog's life. These men are modern heroes. When I am better I will paint them.

> Quoted by Georges Jeanniot, *La Grande Revue* January 1882

Horses Not being in the habit of painting horses, I copied mine from those who know best how to do them.

> Quoted by Berthe Morisot

Literary Imagination (In replying to Mallarmé's invitation to illustrate a new translation of Poe) . . . at the moment it is beyond me. I don't feel capable of doing justice to your needs. I have no model and what is more I have no imagination. I can do nothing worthwhile . . .
. . . certain things which you described to me seem impossible to visualise, amongst other things the woman seen lying in bed under the window. You are terrible, you poets, and it is often impossible to visualise your fantasies. Finally, I'm not well and would be afraid of not meeting your dead-line. If it's possible to bring the matter up again when I get back to Paris, I shall endeavour to attain the elevated status of poet and translator.

> Letters from Versailles, August 1882

I also tried to write, but I did not succeed; I never could do anything but paint.

> Quoted by George Moore

Conciseness Brevity in art is both necessary and elegant. The concise man makes one think; the verbose man is boring. Always try and make yourself more concise . . . In the figure, look for the big light and the big shadow; the rest will follow naturally and there is little else anyway. And then, cultivate your memory, because nature never gives you anything but references. It's like a safety-rail to stop you tumbling into banality . . . you must remain the master and paint what you want to.

Recognition If there were no rewards, I wouldn't invent them: but they exist. And one should have everything that singles you out . . . when possible. It is another weapon. In this beastly life of ours, which is wholly struggle, one is never too well armed. I haven't been decorated? But it is not my fault, and I assure you that I shall be if I can and

that I shall do everything necessary to that end.
To Degas c. 1878, quoted by J. de Nittis *Notes et Souvenirs*
Paris 1895
One year one paints violet and everyone screams, but the next year everyone paints a great deal more violet.
Quoted by George Moore

OTHER ARTISTS ON MANET

Bazille (After Manet's exhibition at Martinet's Gallery, March 1863)
You wouldn't believe how much I have learned from looking at these paintings. One experience like this is worth a whole month's work.

Courbet on *Olympia* (c. 1865)
It is flat, it isn't modelled; like the Queen of Spades on a playing card just out of her bath.

Degas That Manet, as soon as I did dancers, he did them. He always imitated. Manet wasn't thinking about *plein air* when he painted *Le Déjeuner sur l'Herbe*. He never thought about it until he saw Monet's first paintings. He could never do anything but imitate.
You have read how Manet used a black mirror to gauge values. All that is very complicated.
Manet is in despair because he cannot paint atrocious pictures like Duran and be fêted and decorated; he is an artist not by inclination but by force, he is a galley slave chained to the oar.
The Manet (*Bar aux Folies-Bergère*), both clever and stupid, a playing card with no depth, Spanish trompe-l'oeil. (1882)
We never knew how great he was. (1883)

Redon (On the portrait of Zola 1868) Manet, who appears to us especially well-equipped for still life painting, should limit himself to that.

Sickert He was the magnificent painter of the *morceau*. Give me a ham by Manet, a few oysters, a dish of figs... There is hardly any paint. No scaffolding. No groans. No cutting himself with a knife. But on to the canvas spills a living being, with nothing, with a breath. (1908).

George Moore We were taught at the Beaux Arts to consider Manet an absurd person, or else an *épateur* who, not being able to paint like M. Gérôme, determined to astonish.

Matisse Manet was the first painter to translate his emotions directly, thus simplifying the art of painting ... he expressed only what immediately impinged upon his senses.

EXTRACTS FROM CONTEMPORARY CRITICISM

The following extracts are from criticisms of Manet's paintings exhibited in the Salon des Refusés of 1863 and the Salon of 1865. A complete list of Manet's Salon submissions is given on pages 23, 24.

1863 *Le Déjeuner sur l'Herbe*. Originally exhibited under the title *Le Bain*.
A commonplace woman of the demi-monde, as naked as can be, shamelessly lolling between two dandies dressed to the teeth. These latter look like schoolboys on a holiday, perpetrating an outrage to play the man, and I search for the meaning of this unbecoming rebus ... This is a young man's practical joke, a shameful sore not worth exhibiting in this way ...
Louis Étienne

I ought not to omit a remarkable picture of the realist school, a translation of a thought of Giorgione into modern French. Giorgione had conceived the happy idea of a *fête champêtre* in which although the gentlemen were dressed, the ladies were not, but the doubtful morality of the picture is pardoned for the sake of its fine colour... Now some wretched Frenchman has translated this into modern French realism, on a much larger scale, and with the horrible modern French costume instead of the graceful Venetian one ... There are other pictures of the same class, which lead to the inference that the nude, when painted by vulgar men, is inevitably indecent. P. J. Hamerton

After Whistler, the artist who arouses the most discussion is Manet. He, too, is a great painter ... *Le Bain* is very daring ... (but) I can't imagine what made an artist of intelligence and refinement select such an absurd composition, which elegant and charming characters might have justified. Théophile Thoré

There has been a lot of excitement about this young man. Let us be serious. *Le Bain*, the *Majo*, the *Espada* are good sketches, I will grant you. There is a certain verve in the colours, a certain freedom of touch which are in no way commonplace. But then what? Manet thinks himself resolute and powerful. He is only hard. And the amazing thing is that he is as soft as he is hard. That's because he is uncertain about some things and leaves them to chance. Not one detail achieves its final form. I see garments without feeling the anatomical structure which supports them ... boneless fingers ... side whiskers made of strips of black cloth ... What else do I see? The artist's lack of conviction and sincerity. Jules Castagnary

1865 *Olympia* ... the grotesque aspect of his work has two causes: first an almost childish ignorance of the fundamentals of drawing and then, a prejudice in favour of inconceivable vulgarity. Ernest Chesneau

Manet has the distinction of being a danger. But the danger is now passed. *Olympia* can be understood from no point of view, even if you take it for what it is, a puny model stretched out on a sheet. The colour of the flesh is dirty, the modelling non-existent. The shadows are indicated by more or

6 George Moore in the Café de la Nouvelle-Athènes

less large smears of blacking. What's to be said of the negress ... or for the black cat which leaves its ugly footprints on the bed? We would still forgive the ugliness, were it only truthful, carefully studied, heightened by some splendid effect of colour. The least beautiful woman has bones, muscles, skin, and some sort of colour. Here there is nothing, we are sorry to say, but the desire to attract attention at any price. Théophile Gautier

BAUDELAIRE ON MANET

Manet whom people think wild and insane, is simply a very straightforward, unaffected person, as reasonable as can be, but unfortunately touched by romanticism from birth.

Letter to Thoré, 1864

In May 1865 Manet wrote to Baudelaire in Brussels a letter containing the following: 'I could wish that you were here. Insults pour down on me like hail. I should so much like to have your opinions of my paintings, for all this outcry irritates me, and it is evident that someone or other is at fault.' This is an extract from Baudelaire's reply:

I thank you for your good letter which Chorner brought me this morning, as well as for the piece of music...

... I must speak to you of yourself. I must try to show you what you are worth. What you demand is really stupid. *They make fun of you; the jokes aggravate you; no one knows how to do you justice, etc., etc...* Do you think you are the first man put in this predicament? Are you a greater genius than Chateaubriand or Wagner? Yet certainly they were made fun of. They didn't die of it. And not to give you too much cause for pride, I will tell you that these men are examples, each in his own field and in a very rich world; and that you, you are only the first in the decrepitude of your art. I hope you won't be angry with me for treating you so ceremoniously. You are aware of my friendship for you.

I wanted to get a personal impression from this Chorner... and what he told me fits in with what I know of you, and with what some imaginative people say of you: *There are some faults, some failings, a lack of balance, but there is an irresistible charm.* I know all that, I was one of the first to understand it. He added that the painting of the nude woman, with the negress and the cat (is it really a cat?), was far superior to the religious painting. (May 11th.)

Manet has a strong talent, a talent which will resist. But he has a weak character. He seems to me disconsolate and dazed by the shock. I am also struck by the delight of the idiots who think they have ruined him.

Letter to Champfleury, May 25th 1865

ZOLA ON MANET

Since he felt he was getting nowhere by ... painting nature seen through other eyes than his own, quite simply one morning he understood that it was up to him to try to see nature as it is without looking for it in the works and opinions of others. As soon as this idea occurred to him he took anything whatsoever, a person or an object, put it in his studio and began to reproduce it on canvas according to his own ability to see and understand it...

... I am impressed by an inevitable consequence of this exact observation of the law of values. The artist in front of any object at all, lets himself be guided by his eyes which perceive this subject in broad areas of related tones. A head placed against a wall is nothing more than a whitish spot against a greyish background, and the clothing next to the face becomes, for example, a bluish spot beside a whitish spot. In this way the extremely simple arrangement of precise and delicate brushstrokes with almost no detail gives the painting a striking relief at a distance of a few feet... His whole artistic temperament consists in the way his vision is organised...

The first impression produced by a canvas by Manet is a little austere. We are not accustomed to seeing such simple and direct translations of reality... After a few seconds the whole vigorous effect appears, and it is a truly charming experience to contemplate this luminous and serious painting which interprets nature with a tender brutality...

I take this opportunity to denounce the relationship some people have wished to establish between Manet's paintings and Baudelaire's poetry. I know that a warm friendship exists between the poet and the painter, but I believe I can say that the latter has never been guilty of the stupidity committed by others of wishing to put ideas into his paintings. The brief analysis of his talent which I have just given proves how simply he confronts nature. If he assembles several objects or figures he is guided in his choice only by his desire to create fine brush strokes, beautiful oppositions of tone. It is ridiculous to try to make a mystical dreamer out of an artist obedient to such a temperament... He knows neither how to sing, nor to philosophise. He knows how to paint, and that is all.

From Zola's article, 'A new style in painting: M. Edouard Manet'. *Revue du XIXe siecle* Jan Ist. 1867.

Extracts from *Reasons for a Private Exhibition*, the catalogue introduction to Manet's independent exhibition of 1867. It has been variously attributed to Manet himself, to the critic Zacharie Astruc and to Zola, but must at least reflect Manet's feelings.

...one must be able to exhibit what one has done. Without that the artist would be all too easily shut up in a circle from which there is no exit. He would be forced either to stack his canvasses or roll them up in a hayloft.

It is said that official recognition, encouragement, and rewards are actually a guarantee of talent in the eyes of a certain part of the public; they are thereby forewarned in behalf of or against the accepted or rejected works. But on the other hand, the painter is assured that it is the spontaneous impression of this same public which motivates the chilly welcome the various juries give his canvas. In these circumstances the artist has been advised to wait. To wait for what? Until there is no longer a jury? He has preferred to settle the question with the public. The artist does not say today, 'Come and see faultless work', but 'Come and see sincere work'...

Manet has never wished to protest. It is rather against him that people have protested, because there is a traditional system of teaching form, technique, and appearances in painting, and because those who have been brought up according to such principles do not acknowledge any other. From that they derive their naive intolerance. Outside their formulas nothing is valid, and they become not only critics, but adversaries, and active adversaries...

Manet has always recognised talent wherever he found it and has presumed neither to overthrow earlier painting nor to make it new. He has merely tried to be himself and not someone else.

Notes on the illustrations

All works are oil on canvas unless otherwise stated. The JW or Guérin references given at the foot of most entries refer respectively to the catalogue numbers in:
JAMOT, Paul and WILDENSTEIN, Georges: *Manet* Vol. 1 (Paris, 1932) and GUÉRIN, Marcel: *L'Oeuvre Gravé de Manet* (Paris, 1944)

THE BLACK AND WHITE ILLUSTRATIONS

Figure 2 *Study for Olympia*. 1863. Red chalk. Bibliothèque Nationale, Paris.
This drawing from life is one of several studies made before Manet's final decision to borrow Olympia's pose from a Titian painting (see plates 15 and 16). Areas of light and shadow are schematically simplified in a manner closely related to his painting style.

Figure 3 *Profile Portrait of Baudelaire*. 1862. Etching (2nd state). 4¼×3½ in (11×9 cm.). Bibliothèque Nationale, Paris.
Manet's relationship with Baudelaire is discussed in the Introduction and illustrated in the appendix of contemporary writings. The curvilinearity of the monogram is reminiscent of the manner of Whistler, whom Manet met in 1861. Both were close acquaintances of Degas, both were championed first by Baudelaire and then by Mallarmé and they were fellow victims of hostility at the 1863 Salon des Refusés. (see note to plate 9). Their painting in the 1860s was moving in the same direction, with subject matter taking an increasingly passive role. (Guérin 31)

Figure 4 Marcantonio Raimondi. *Engraving after Raphael's 'Judgement of Paris'* (detail of the River Gods). Metropolitan Museum of Art, New York. Rogers Fund, 1919.
See note to plate 9.

Figure 5 *Le Rendez-vous des Chats*. 1868. Lithograph. 17¼× 13¼ in. (43.5×33.5 cm.). Museum of Fine Arts, Boston. Gift of W. G. R. Allen.
Cats appear frequently in Manet's graphic work as well as in several paintings. They reveal his understanding and enjoyment of feline movement. In black and white media Manet felt more free to experiment with bold tonal patterns. This experience possibly contributed to his developed style of painting in the 1860s. (Guérin 74)

Figure 6 *George Moore in the Café de la Nouvelle-Athènes*. c. 1879. Oil sketch. 25½×31 in. (65×79 cm.). M. Knoedler and Co., New York.
The Café de la Nouvelle-Athènes became a popular meeting place for artists and writers in the late 1870s: Manet and Degas were the principal figures in the circle, their chairs always reserved, their presence and opinions always greatly respected. Moore, a young Irish art-student-turned-writer and critic became a devoted admirer of Manet. (JW 337)

THE COLOUR PLATES

Plate 1 *Portrait of The Artist's Parents*. Dated 1860. 43¼× 35½ in. (11×90 cm.). Rouart Collection, Paris.
Exhibited at the Salon of 1861. Manet's family was respectable, conventional and fairly prosperous. His father, a distinguished magistrate, intended that Edouard—the eldest of three sons—should read law and (the familiar story) only agreed with reluctance to let him become an artist; and then only through the respectable channels of the Ecole des Beaux Arts in Paris. This last condition Manet would not have wanted otherwise. (JW 37)

Plate 2 *The Absinthe Drinker*. 1858/9. 71¼×41¾ in. (181× 106 cm.). Ny Carlsberg Glyptotek, Copenhagen.

Rejected at the Salon of 1859. Manet's ex-master Thomas Couture said of it, 'only another absinthe drinker could have painted so foolishly'; this remark ended their strained relationship. Manet said about the painting's rejection by the Jury (it was his first submission to the Salon): 'I painted a Parisian character whom I'd studied in Paris, and I executed it with the technical simplicity I had discovered in Velasquez. No one understands it. If I painted a Spanish type it would be more comprehensible'. This is of course what Manet did (plate 3) and it was comprehended.

The sitter was a rag-and-bone man who frequented the Louvre called Colardet. Manet was probably attracted not by the sordidness of the subject or a sense of social comment, but by the eccentric picturesqueness of Colardet as a pictorial motif (he re-used it in *The Old Musician* (plate 4).

(JW 24)

Plate 3 *The Guitarist*. (Also known as the *Spanish Guitarist*). Dated 1860. 57×44 in. (146×114 cm.). Metropolitan Museum of Art, New York. Gift of William Church Osborne, 1949. Exhibited at the Salon in 1861 where it was accorded an honourable mention. Manet shared the current Parisian taste for all things Spanish and made several paintings and drawings of a troupe of Spanish entertainers who performed at the Paris Hippodrome in 1862. This taste complemented his early interest in Spanish painting. Presumably the picturesque and topical novelty of the subject accounted for the painting's success. A group of young painters (including Fantin Latour and Legros) were sufficiently attracted to visit Manet in his studio, and some critics wrote favourably of his fluent breadth of handling.

(JW 40)

Plate 4 *The Old Musician*. Dated 1862. 74×94¼ in. (186 ×247 cm.). National Gallery of Art, Washington, D.C. Chester Dale Collection.

Exhibited at Martinet's Gallery in 1863 and in Manet's independent exhibition of 1867. Jamot says that the subject was inspired by some street beggars of the derelict Rue Guyot, Paris. But even if that was where the inspiration lay, the painting is essentially an allegory of *la vie moderne* based on a much wider experience. The similarity of the general disposition of the figures and setting to Velasquez' painting *Los Borrachos* has long been recognised (see note on plate 25). The figures include Manet's own *Absinthe Drinker* (cf. plate 2) and the two central children have been likened to figures from Watteau (left) and Velasquez (right). Manet assembles them as if in a photomontage or collage, paying scant lip-service to conventions of spatial and narrative unity.

(JW 44)

Plate 5 *La Musique aux Tuileries* (Concert in the Tuileries Gardens). Dated 1862. 30×46½ in. (76×199 cm.). National Gallery, London.
First exhibited at Martinet's Gallery in 1863. Antonin Proust's memoirs include the following comments about Manet at this period:

Each day he used to go to the Tuileries gardens from two o'clock until four, making studies on the spot under the trees, of the children playing and of their nannies lounging in small groups. Baudelaire was always with him then... A small circle of admirers used to form around him. The café Tortoni was the restaurant where he ate lunch before going to the Tuileries, and when he returned to this café between five and six, his drawings were passed around for the admiring comments of this little court. Manet could believe for a moment that in this very France, where—as Voltaire said—'le succès seul a du succès', he was already on the path to glory.

The setting of this painting is the public park of the Tuileries in Paris, a fashionable meeting place where music was played under the trees. The recognisable portraits are of members of Manet's family and its social circle and various other personalities with whom he was in contact at the time: the critics Gautier, Champfleury and Astruc, Baudelaire and Lord Taylor, painter friends like Fantin-Latour, and, to the extreme left, Manet himself. This self-documentation is uncharacteristic and short-lived and in it there is an echo of *l'Atelier* (1855), Courbet's self-allegory, but as an ambitions attempt to compose a fashionable and serious period piece it is better compared to Seurat's... *la Grande Jatte* (1884-6). (JW 38)

Plate 6 *The Street Singer*. c. 1862-3. 68½×46½ in. (175× 118 cm.). Museum of Fine Art, Boston. On anonymous loan. Exhibited at Martinet's Gallery in 1863 and in Manet's independent exhibition of 1867. The painting was inspired when Manet saw a chanteuse leaving a Paris café. When the woman refused to pose for him, he used Victorine Meurent as his model. She was not an experienced professional, but became Manet's favourite model in the 1860s. She also posed for plates 7, 9, 14, 18, 20 (?) and 33. (JW 45)

Plate 7 *Mlle Victorine in the Costume of an Espada*. c. 1862-3. 65×50¼ in. (166×129 cm.). Metropolitan Museum of Art, New York. Bequest of Mrs. H. O. Havemeyer, 1929, The H. O. Havemeyer Collection.
Exhibited at the Salon des Refusés of 1863 and in Manet's independent exhibition of 1867. A pendant picture (*Young man in the Costume of a Majo* JW 52) which was also shown at the Salon de Refusés, is dated 1862. The importance of the painting in the development of Manet's style is suggested in the introduction. (JW 51)

Plate 8 *Le Déjeuner sur l'Herbe* (Luncheon on the Grass) study? 1862-3. 35¼×45¾ in. (89.5×116 cm.). Courtauld Institute Galleries London.
Douglas Cooper (*The Courtauld Collection*, London, 1954. Cat.

No. 32) suggests that this might be a copy of the large painting rather than a study for it. (JW 78)

Plates 9 and 10 *Le Déjeuner sur l'Herbe* (Luncheon on the Grass) and detail. 1862-3. 84¾×106⅜ in. (214×270 cm.). Musée du Louvre, Paris.
Originally titled *Le Bain* in the Salon des Refusés catalogue; but according to Duret it was already widely known by its present title. Listed in Manet's 1871 inventory as *La Partie Carrée* (The Foursome).

Proust recalls that while a student Manet had considered the problem of the place of the nude in paintings of modern life: 'I'm well aware that you can't get a model to pose naked in the streets, but there are fields and—in the summer at least—one can make nude studies in the country'. In the summer of 1862 during a walk along the banks of the Seine Manet returned to the subject in saying to Proust that he wanted to reinterpret the subject of Giorgione's painting *La Fête Champêtre* in terms of real sunlight and atmosphere. (He had copied the Giorgione painting in the Louvre as a student).

In fact the painting was executed in Manet's studio and the three principal figures were posed for by (left to right) Victorine Meurent, Manet's brother-in-law Ferdinand Leenhoff; and Eugene Manet, his brother. It is hardly *a plein air* painting and it often cited as an ancestor to the figures in landscape compositions of the later Renoir, of Cézanne, Seurat, Matisse, Picasso and the Cubists, none of which has very much to do with spontaneous open-air naturalism. This aspect of the painting is also mentioned in the introduction.

The pose of the main group was borrowed from an engraving after Raphael's drawing *The Judgement of Paris* (see figure 4), with suitable modifications of dress and accessories. This source was first noticed in 1864.

Manet sent the painting to the 1863 Salon where it was

rejected by the jury. It was then shown in the *Salon des Re-fusés*, a special exhibition hastily arranged in 1863 at the instigation of the Emperor. When the Salon jury's selection had been announced—some weeks before the Salon was due to open—it was seen that an unusually large number of paintings, over four thousand, had been rejected. The Emperor's decision was in theory to appease the storm of protests by inviting all the rejected artists to exhibit their paintings in a separate Salon. But reading between the lines of the official announcement (which proposed 'to leave the public as judge of the legitimacy of these complaints'), it is clear that the real intention was to prove the jury's wisdom and the rejected artists took up the invitation at their peril. When the Salon des Refusés opened, two weeks after the official Salon opening, the public and critics took the cue and greeted the paintings with abuse and ridicule. Napoleon III is reported to have set the tone by striking at *Le Déjeuner* with his riding whip (accounts of this incident vary considerably). Examples of the criticism are quoted on pages 26, 27, and briefly discussed in the introduction. Whistler's *The White Girl* (1862) shared the limelight of notoriety with this painting.

(A smaller Salon des Refusés was held the following year, but attracted little attention and was never repeated.)

(JW 79)

Plate 11 *The Dead Christ with Angels*. 1864. 68⅛×61 in. (175×155 cm.). Metropolitan Museum of Art, New York. Bequest of Mrs H. O. Havemeyer. The H. O. Havemeyer Collection.
Exhibited in the Salon of 1864. One of the two religious subjects painted by Manet in the 1860s; thereafter he abandoned the attempt to reconcile such content with his new technique. (Although Proust reveals Manet's later ambition to paint a Crucifixion, 'the foundation ... the poem, of

humanity.') Much contemporary criticism concentrated upon the indecorous treatment of the subject matter. Gautier complained of the un-celestial angels 'the artist hasn't tried to raise them above a vulgar level', and wondered of the body of Christ if a cadavre so far gone can ever be resurrected. Others criticised Manet's error in painting Christ's wound on his left side instead of his right; in a gouache after the painting (given to Zola and now in the Louvre) Manet corrected this.

(JW 85)

Plate 12 *Women at The Races*. 1864/5. 16½×12½ in. (42×32 cm.). Cincinnati Art Museum, Ohio.
Bought at the posthumous sale of 1884 by the Impressionist painter Caillebotte and afterwards in the collection of the German painter Max Liebermann who owned several of Manet's paintings. The popularity of Manet's work in Germany was more responsible for the advent of Impressionism there than was the influence of the true Impressionists.

One of the series of racecourse pictures presumed to have been painted in 1864 when Manet worked at Longchamp (of which plate 13 is the outstanding work). Degas claimed to have invented the genre—he first painted racecourse motifs around 1862—but the precedent of Gericault's interest in the subject is not insignificant. One of a later group of racing subjects by Manet (*Race at the Bois de Boulogne*, 1872, JW 359) certainly owes much to Géricault and/or English sporting prints. For Manet the racecourse was a valid part of contemporary life and he was not over-concerned with originality of motif.

(JW 80)

Plate 13 *Races At Longchamp*. 1864. 17¼×33¼ in. (44×84.5 cm.). Art Institute, Chicago. Potter Palmer collection.
This is the most impressionist painting of Manet's of the 1860s, the most extreme example of Manet's use of rapid execution to evoke a feeling of movement and transience.

This is even more apparent in his drawings of the subject.
(JW 202)

Plates 14 and 16 (detail). *Olympia*. Dated 1863. 51⅛ × 74¾ in. (130 × 190 cm.). Musée du Louvre, Paris.
Exhibited at the Salon of 1865 and in Manet's independent exhibition of 1867. Manet is said to have regarded it as his greatest work and certainly many of his friends and champions did. In his inventory of 1871 he valued it at 20,000 fr. and it was withdrawn from the posthumous sale of 1884 when it failed to reach 10,000 fr. In 1889, after rumours of its purchase by an American collector, Claude Monet organised a private subscription to purchase the painting for the French nation. About 20,000 fr. was raised (subscribers included Degas, Duret, Lautrec, Mallarmé, Puvis de Chavannes, Renoir and Rodin) and the painting entered the Luxembourg Palace in 1890. Gauguin painted his copy of it in the same year. It was transferred to the Louvre in 1907.

The significance of the title presented problems to those contemporaries and critics who felt that the subject begged for an anecdotal interpretation. (Clarétie for example asked, 'What is this odalisque with a yellow belly... who represents Olympia? What Olympia? A courtesan no doubt'. *l'Artiste* May 15th). The name Olympia was in fact suggested by Zacharie Astruc, just before the painting was shown at the Salon (i.e. nearly two years after its execution). Baudelaire who was in Brussels at the time, referred to it simply as 'the painting of the nude woman with the negress and the cat'. When the painting was exhibited Manet used the first five lines of a long poem by Astruc as a commentary (on the label, according to Hamilton; in the Salon catalogue, according to Jamot).

Neither the name nor the poem had anything to do with the painting's conception; Manet probably accepted it almost on impulse as a suitably distinctive but ambiguous

identification which would distinguish it from the traditional Venus motif. The principal compositional source was Titian's *Urbino Venus* (see note to plate 15), but others have been suggested including paintings by Ingres and Jalabert and Goya's *Naked Maja*. Criticisms of the painting in 1865 denounced Manet as the disciple of the ugly and repulsive and his paintings as offensive eccentricities. Examples are given on page 27. The two main objections concerned unorthodox technique and indecent subject matter. The innovations of Manet's revolutionary technique are discussed in the introduction: the public was totally unprepared for it and could hardly have been expected to understand Manet's intention. In view of the hostile reception of *Le Déjeuner sur l'Herbe* in 1863, a distortion of his intention was almost inevitable. The fact that Manet did not submit this painting to the 1864 Salon, as he could have done, suggests that he was aware of this.

The indecency charges must arise chiefly from the fixed and unabashed stare of this unidealised unclothed girl: she was not far enough removed from reality, without the coyly averted glance of Titian's Venus which might have made her more acceptable. Cabanel's artfully seductive *Birth of Venus*, shown at the 1863 Salon, had been purchased by the Emperor and brought its creator promotion in the Légion d'Honneur.

Whether one sees in Manet's submission of this painting to the Salon an element of naiveté or deliberate provocation, or simply the strength of his convictions, the suggestions of immorality were no more than protests against its total lack of eroticism. There is an interesting suggestion that Courbet's painting *La Femme au Perroquet*, a sprawling female nude which enjoyed a reasonable success at the 1866 Salon was Courbet's answer to *Olympia*; and that Manet's own *La Femme au Perroquet* (plate 18) was a deliberate and highly tasteful corrective to Courbet's uncouth misunderstanding of

Olympia. This possible dialogue between the two artists may go back further if, as has been suggested, Manet's *Déjeuner sur l'Herbe* (plate 9) was partly inspired by Courbet's *Girls on the Banks of the Seine* (1856). (JW 82)

Plate 15 *Copy after Titian's Urbino Venus*. c. 1856. 9½×14½ in. (24×37 cm.). Rouart Collection, Paris.
Previously belonged to Manet's brother Eugène and his wife (Berthe Morisot). Ernest Rouart married their daughter.
Presumably executed during Manet's second visit to Italy in 1856. The original is in the Uffizi, Florence. Manet made many copies after the old masters, including other works by Titian, Tintoretto, Velasquez and his followers, Rembrandt, Brouwer, Delacroix and others. This copy was the starting point for the final composition of *Olympia* (plate 14) in 1863 and may even have suggested the whole idea of the painting to him. Olympia's pose, the bracelet, the inclusion of a servant and an animal, the drapery, the vertical division of the background, are all direct references to the Titian painting. The originality of *Olympia* lies in the reinterpretation of the borrowed motif. (JW 4)

Plate 17 *Portrait of Zacharie Astruc*. Dated 1864. 35½×65 in. (90×116 cm.). Kunsthalle, Bremen.
Exhibited in Manet's independent exhibition of 1867. Astruc, amateur painter, sculptor, musician, poet, critic suggested the title of *Olympia* (see note to plate 14). The screened division of the background, with its inverted quotation from Titian's *Urbino Venus* is presumably an acknowledgment of this. Astruc had written a strong defence of Manet during the Salon of 1863. (JW 103)

Plate 18 *La Femme au Perroquet* (Woman with a Parrot). c. 1866. 72¾×52 in. (185×132 cm.). Metropolitan Museum of Art, New York. Gift of Erwin Davies, 1889.

Exhibited in Manet's independent exhibition of 1867 and in the Salon of 1868.
The model was Victorine Meurent. The picturesque charm of the subject is part of Manet's feeling for his period. In the assured fluency of his painting at this time, this subjective and dated taste is carried along by the marriage of his effortless colour sense with his totally unmannered execution. (JW 132)

Plate 19 *The Philosopher*. 1865-6. 74¼×43 in. (188.6×109.3 cm.). Art Institute of Chicago. A. A. Munger Collection.
This was painted immediately after Manet's trip to Spain (August 1865) and the debt to Velasquez is abundantly evident in its subject, composition, treatment of space and in the cool clarity of its colour and execution. (JW 112)

Plate 20 *Le Fifre* (The Fifer). 1865-6. 63×38½ in. (160×98 cm.). Musée du Louvre, Paris.
Painted in the winter of 1865-6 for the 1866 Salon, at which it was rejected. Included in Manet's independent exhibition of 1867. Commandant Lejosne (either a friend or relative, biographers disagree) lent Manet a young cadet musician to pose for the picture; later he supplied models for the *Execution of Maximilian* (plates 21-23).
Jamot suggested that Victorine Meurent also posed for the painting. It is painted with all the hope and confidence that Manet drew from seeing Velasquez's art in Spain (1865). Compare it with plate 7 for the greater resolution of his style (especially in space/tone relationships) between the years 1862 and 1866. (JW 126)

Plates 21 and 22 *The Execution of Maximilian* (Two fragments). c. 1867. National Gallery, London. The signature on plate 22 is not original. Plate 21 *The Firing Squad* 75×63 in.

(190×160 cm.). Plate 22 *Soldier Examining His Rifle* 39× 23¼ in. (99×59 cm.).
These are two fragments of a very large painting (about 9×10 feet). Two smaller fragments are also in the National Gallery. Apparently Manet rolled the canvas up after completing or abandoning it, and it suffered from damp and cracking. Later the salvagable pieces were cut out, possibly by Manet's family after his death. Three surviving pieces were bought by Degas who remounted them together on another canvas and had them photographed. They were bought by the National Gallery at the posthumous sale of Degas' collection in 1918. (See note to plate 23.)   (JW 139)

Plate 23 *The Execution of Maximilian.* c. 1868. 99¼×120 in. (252×305 cm.). Stadtische Kunsthalle, Mannheim.
Exhibited in America 1879-80. This is Manet's final version of the subject and is dated 19th June, 1867. A small sketch in Copenhagen (JW 141), is obviously a study for this painting. The five versions were executed between Autumn 1867 and the end of 1868, probably in the following sequence: 1 A painting now in Boston (about 6½×8½ feet. JW 138). 2 The National Gallery version. 3 An undated lithograph (Guérin 73). 4 The Copenhagen sketch. 5 The Mannheim version.
The history of the subject
The Austrian Ferdinand-Joseph Maximilian, the 'marionette Emperor' of Mexico, had accepted the French-sponsored invitation to that throne in 1864 when he was 32. His execution and that of two of his generals (Miramon and Meija) at Queretaro on 19th June, 1867 was the climax of a popular rising led by Juarez. The French Emperor Napoleon III had declared war against Juarez in 1866 and supplied French troops to keep Maximilian's throne intact but suddenly withdrew them to meet commitments in Europe. During August, September and October eye-witness reports

of the execution were published in Paris. They were pathos-laden accounts giving precise details of dress, distance setting and spectators. (A photograph of the firing party was published in *Le Figaro* on 11th of August.) Parisians felt a great sympathy for the heroic tragedy of Maximilian as well as considerable revulsion against the element of betrayal in Napoleon's politics. Manet's lithograph was still being suppressed on political grounds as late as 1869.
His own attitude to the subject is discussed in the introduction.
During the series Manet altered settings, uniforms and other details as new facts came to light. The faces of the condemned men were probably based on photographs. The firing squad was modelled by a group of soldiers in Manet's studio (the photograph of the firing squad shows that the Mexicans' uniform was almost identical with that of the French army). The composition of the figures is obviously borrowed from Goya's painting *The 3rd May 1808* which Manet must have seen in Madrid. This is a characteristic example of Manet's lifting of ready-made pictorial devices to suit the particular context in hand: he used the motif of the firing squad again (identical but in reverse) for a study of the Paris barricades in 1871.
The final version of the subject is an extraordinary patchwork of ready-made material, both factual and pictorial. This only holds together because when Manet was actually painting it, he was no longer interested in the assembly of the material or its meaning, but only in the subtle adjustment of tones and the harmony of his colour relationships.
Sandblad (see book list page 22) illustrates some of the documentary material available to Manet.   (JW 140)

Plate 24 *Portrait of Théodore Duret.* Dated 1868. 17×13¾ in. (43×35 cm.). Petit Palais, Paris.
In an account of this painting Duret describes the last minute

inclusion of the stool and still life after the figure was finished. In colour and execution the painting is typical of the late '60s.

Manet first met Duret in 1865 in the dining room of a Madrid hotel where, after a violent disagreement about the quality of the food (Duret had just arrived from Portugal, starving and prepared to eat anything, Manet was discriminatingly fresh from the *haute cuisine* of Paris), they introduced themselves and became close friends. Duret was a young critic, perceptive and widely travelled (he was probably Manet's only acquaintance to have visited Japan). His first book, *Les Peintres Français en 1867* (Paris, 1867) included a thoughtful and largely favourable discussion of Manet. He later came to consider Manet as one of the real 'inventors' among painters. (JW 147)

Plate 25 *Portrait of Emile Zola.* 1867-8. 57×43⅝ in. (190 ×110 cm.). Musée du Louvre, Paris.
Shown in the Salon of 1868. The background of the portrait shows a Japanese screen, an Utamaro print, a photograph (? or perhaps a print) of *Olympia* and a part of Goya's print after the Velasquez painting *Los Borrachos*. On the table is the magazine in which Zola had published his important article on Manet: Manet's name on the cover serves as the painting's signature. Because of this very personal programme of the motif some writers have spoken of it as more of a self-portrait than that of Zola. It was painted in Manet's studio, so the various properties which lucidly summarise his artistic sources were almost certainly in Manet's own possession. Zola's perceptive criticism of Manet is discussed in the text and extracts are quoted on pages 28, 29. (JW 146)

Plate 26 *Still Life with Salmon.* c. 1869. 28¼×36¼ in. (72 ×92 cm.). Shelburne Museum, Shelburne, Vermont. On loan from the Electra Havemeyer Webb Fund Inc.

There are a large number of still life paintings in Manet's oeuvre and Redon once suggested that he should paint nothing else: this characteristically astute criticism recognises that Manet's painterly qualities achieved their fullest realisation when unfettered by considerations of literary content. The motif of this superb example seems related to the still life in plate 27. (JW 168)

Plates 27 and 28 *Le Déjeuner à l'Atelier* (Luncheon in the Studio) and detail. 1868. 47¼×60⅝ in. (120×151 cm.). Neue Staatsgalerie, Munich.
Exhibited at the Salon of 1869 and in Brussels in the same year. The male sitters were Léon Leenhoff (centre), who it has been suggested was Manet's son, born before his marriage, and the painter Rousselin. The peculiar qualities of Manet's art in the 1860s are discussed at some length in the introduction. This is a masterpiece of that period. The motif itself is distinctly unmemorable and the role of the figures a passive one (the bland impersonal paint emphasises this) but the balance achieved in the tones and the restrained colour endows the painting with a very distinctive identity. The total and self sufficient accord of the painting's values has a quality of absoluteness that makes it a landmark of 19th century painting and a milestone in the evolution of modern art's conceptions. (JW 149)

Plate 29 *Le Balcon* (The Balcony). 1868-9. 66½×48½ in. (169×123 cm.). Musée du Louvre, Paris.
Exhibited in the 1869 Salon. The principal sitters were, left to right, Berthe Morisot, Antoine Guillemet and Fanny Claus. Morisot wrote of Manet's Salon entries in 1869: 'These paintings give as always the impression of a fruit that grows wild and is perhaps still unripe. But they certainly don't dissatisfy me ... (in them) I am more strange than ugly. It seems that the epithet "femme fatale" has gone

the round of the inquisitive.' The composition has been compared to Goya's well-known painting of Majas sitting on a balcony. The subtleties of composition and the selective control of colour are wholly personal to Manet.   (JW 150)

Plate 30 *Portrait of Berthe Morisot*. Dated 1872. 21¾ × 15 in. (55 × 38 cm.). Rouart Collection, Paris.
The Impressionist painter Berthe Morisot first met Manet in 1867, and in 1868 became his pupil. In 1874 she married his brother Eugène. She sat for Manet on several occasions (see plate 29). She usually dressed in black and white and this may have encouraged him to use her as a model. Their friendship strengthened the contacts between Manet and Impressionist ideas.   (JW 208)

Plate 31 *The Outlet of Boulogne Harbour*. 29⅛ × 36⅝ in. (74 × 93 cm.). Art Institute of Chicago. Potter Palmer Collection. Exhibited in Manet's independent exhibition, 1867.
The almost Japanese economy of execution is reminiscent of Whistler's Thames pictures.   (JW 92)

Plate 32 *Clair de Lune au Port de Boulogne* (Moonlight on Boulogne Harbour). 1869. 32¼ × 39⅜ ins. (82 × 100 cm.). Musée du Louvre, Paris.
According to JW it was painted from the window of a Boulogne hotel. One of several seascapes and landscapes of around 1870 in which Manet imposed his simplified tone and colour upon potentially Impressionist subjects.   (JW 159)

Plate 33 *The Railway*. 1873. 36⅝ × 44⅛ in. (93 × 112 cm.). National Gallery of Art, Washington, D.C. Gift of Horace Havemeyer in memory of his mother Louisine W. Havemeyer. The showing of this painting at the Salon of 1874, the year of the first Impressionist group exhibition, helped the public to associate Manet with the younger artists. But the citation

of it by some historians as an ancestor of Monet's railway series seems like special pleading. Despite the title, the picture is only slightly involved with urban reality. It is clearly a studio painting and its individuality depends upon the play of the flatly painted figures against the severe grid of the railings.   (JW 231)

Plate 34 *Le Bon Bock* (A Good Beer). 1872-3. 37 × 32⅝ in. (94 × 83 cm.). Philadelphia Museum of Art, Pennsylvania. Mr and Mrs Carroll S. Tyson Collection.
Shown at the 1873 Salon. After the 'honourable mention' of *The Guitarist* in 1861 this was Manet's only really popular public success. The anecdotal joviality of the motif and the more highly finished execution must have contributed to it: the two main criticisms previously levelled against Manet were thus answered, perhaps consciously. The relation to Dutch genre painting (Manet had just returned from a visit to Holland during which he had developed a deep admiration for Frans Hals) was noticed by contemporaries and has been commented on by most writers since. His friend Alfred Stevens annoyed Manet with the comment, 'he is drinking Haarlem beer'. The jury made no award, but the seal of public approval was set by the use of the motif as a *tableau vivant* in a revue at the Théâtre du Château d'Eau. The actor of the role wrote respectfully to Manet inviting criticism of the authenticity of his performance.   (JW 213)

Plate 35 *Argenteuil*. Dated 1874. 58⅝ × 51½ ins. (149 × 131 cm.). Musée des Beaux Arts, Tournai.
Shown at the 1875 Salon. Plates 35 to 37 are typical of Manet's Impressionist period of the early 1870s. They were at least partly painted on the spot; the skidding brushwork is freely broken and the colour is bright and unrestrained. The best of them capture the open-air radiance of the works of Monet, Renoir and Sisley (plates 36 and 37 were painted

during the summer of 1874 while Manet was staying with Monet and his wife at Argenteuil). Nevertheless there are characteristic differences: the dominant role of the figure, the more localised colour and the controlling intervals of Manet's use of black and grey. (JW 241)

Plate 36 *The Seine at Argenteuil*. Dated 1874. 24½×40½ in. (62×103 cm.). The Dowager Lady Aberconway, London. See note to plate 36. (JW 242)

Plate 37 *Venice, the Grand Canal* 1874. 18⅞×22½ in. (48×57 cm.). Shelburne Museum, Shelburne, Vermont. On loan from the Electra Havemeyer Webb Fund Inc.
Painted during a visit to Venice in August 1874. It was bought by the painter James Tissot in 1875. (JW 247)

Plate 38 *La Servante de Bocks* (The Beer Waitress). 1878-9. 38¼×30½ ins. (98×77 cm.). National Gallery, London.
This was originally part of a large painting which was cut in two. Both parts were then extensively reworked. The other half (JW 314) is signed and dated 1878. It is one of several café interiors painted in the 1870s. Coupled with the close-up viewpoint and cutting of figures it owes something to the 'key-hole philosophy' of Degas' impressionism. There are music-hall and female nude motifs which seem to confirm this source of influence. Degas himself had no doubt about it. (See contemporary writings page 26). (JW 335)

Plate 39 *Portrait of Mallarmé*. 1876. 10⅝×13¾ in. (26×34 cm.). Musée du Louvre, Paris.
Stéphane Mallarmé (1842-98) was closely associated with the visual arts throughout his career, a friend of Whistler and champion of Gauguin. He first met Manet in 1874. Although Mallarmé's reputation as a writer was as yet unmade, and consequently his favourable criticism carried little public weight, their ten years of close friendship meant much to Manet in terms of moral support. His taste for Manet's painting was, as one might expect, for the musical and indefinable expressiveness of the colour harmonies: he wrote of Manet's exquisite nuances of black. His general conception of painting was that 'the painter should paint not the thing itself, but the effect it produces' and he recognised as invalid the orthodox insistence upon 'finish': 'What is an unfinished work if all its elements are in accord, and if it possesses a charm which could easily be broken by an additional touch?' (1874).

In 1875 Manet made illustrations for Mallarmé's translation of Poe's *The Raven* and in 1876 four more for his *L'Aprèsmidi d'un Faune*. (JW 265)

Plate 40 *Portrait of Clemenceau*. c. 1879-80. 37×29⅛ in. (94×74 cm.). Musée du Louvre, Paris.
Clemenceau (1841-1929), one of several political figures who sat for Manet, was too busy for the painting to be completed. Jamot says it was done in one sitting. (JW 372)

Plate 41 *La Sultane*. c. 1870-5? 36¼×28¾ in. (92×73 cm.). Bührle Collection, Zurich.
Previous dating of this picture has varied between 1871 (JW) and 1876 (Duret). Douglas Cooper (Bührle Collection Exhibition catalogue, Edinburgh 1961, No. 14) suggests c. 1872 on stylistic grounds, but pictures it most resembles both in style and subject (a gouache *Odalisque* (Louvre, Guérin 64) and the *Bathers* (plate 42) are also undated and very difficult to place. Both this painting and the *Bathers* have a tough vigour of execution which rises above Manet's facile impressionist technique and the charm of his society portraits. (JW 200)

Plate 42 *Bathers*. c. 1870-5? 52×38½ in. (132×98 cm.). Museo de Arte, São Paulo, Brazil.
Unfinished and little more than a sketch, this represents a more informal and uninhibited statement of the theme of

le *Déjeuner sur l'Herbe* of 1862-3. As a student Manet had expressed concern about the place of the nude in paintings of modern life (see note to plate 9). (JW 264)

Plate 43 *In the Conservatory*. Dated 1879. 45¼×59 in. (115 ×150 cm.). Exhibited in the 1879 Salon. Staatliche Museen, National Gallery, Berlin-Dahlem.
This painting and plate 44 are the most complete of Manet's contemporary figure subjects of the later '70s. (JW 296)

Plate 44 *Chez le Père Lathuile*. Dated 1879. 36⅜×44⅛ in. (92×112 cm.). Musée des Beaux Arts, Tournai.
Shown in the 1880 Salon. Originally subtitled *In the open air*, and painted *in situ*, this painting always ranks highly in the estimation of those writers who see the 1870s as the period of Manet's major achievement in reconciling his concern for the figure with the Impressionists' vision and technique. (JW 325)

Plate 45 *Portrait of a Young Woman* 1880. 22⅛×18⅛ in. (56×46 cm.). Pastel. Musée du Louvre, Paris.
A good example of the sweet charm of his later fashionable female portraits, perhaps owing something in its soft diffusion to the portraiture of Renoir. Between them they created a genre for generations of studio photographers and pastel-wielding academicians. Manet used pastel increasingly in his last years, partly because of ill-health: he found it easier to use. His pastels form an easy, sometimes frivolous, sometimes sparkling cul-de-sac outside his main oeuvre. (JW 418)

Plate 46 *Nana*. Dated 1877. 59×45⅝ in. (150×116 cm.). Kunsthalle, Hamburg.
Rejected at the Salon of 1877. Zola's novel of the same title had not yet been published, but Manet might well have known of it.
The model was a renowned courtesan specially chosen by Manet for a subject whose anecdotal emphasis is unusual.

It is possible that he was provoking the predictable refusal of the painting 'on moral grounds' by the 1877 Salon jury. It was exhibited instead in Giroux's shop, where it attracted crowds and policemen. (JW 275)

Plate 47 *Le Bar aux Folies-Bergère* (Study). 1881-2. 18½× 22 in. (47×56 cm.). Stedelijk Museum, Amsterdam. On loan from Private Collection.
This painted study was probably based on drawings made on the spot. Some of the foreground details have been re-touched by another hand. (JW 466)

Plate 48 *Le Bar aux Folies-Bergère*. 1881-2. 37½×51 in. (96×130 cm.). Courtauld Institute Galleries, London.
Dated 1882, it was shown in the Salon of that year. The model was a barmaid who posed in Manet's studio standing behind a table laden with bottles, fruit, etc. Georges Jean-niot, who visited Manet while he was working on this paint-ing, described what he saw. Manet sat in a chair since he could no longer stand without a stick. 'I took a chair behind him and watched him work. Although he was painting from the model, Manet didn't copy nature at all: I watched his masterly simplifications. The head of the model took shape, but it wasn't achieved by following nature. Everything was epitomised: the tones were clearer, the colours more alive, the values more related. All of these were united in a subtle, blonde harmony'. (JW 467)

Plate 49 *Self Portrait*. 1879. 32⅝×26⅜ in. (83×67 cm.). Estate of the late Jakob Goldschmidt, New York.
It is difficult to believe that this image represents the same man as the self-confident *flâneur* of the '60s (see frontispiece), or the poised elegant figure described by George Moore. The only other known self-portrait (JW 295), also of the late 1870s, is even less assured in character. (JW 294)

2

3

4

5

6

8

9

10

12

13

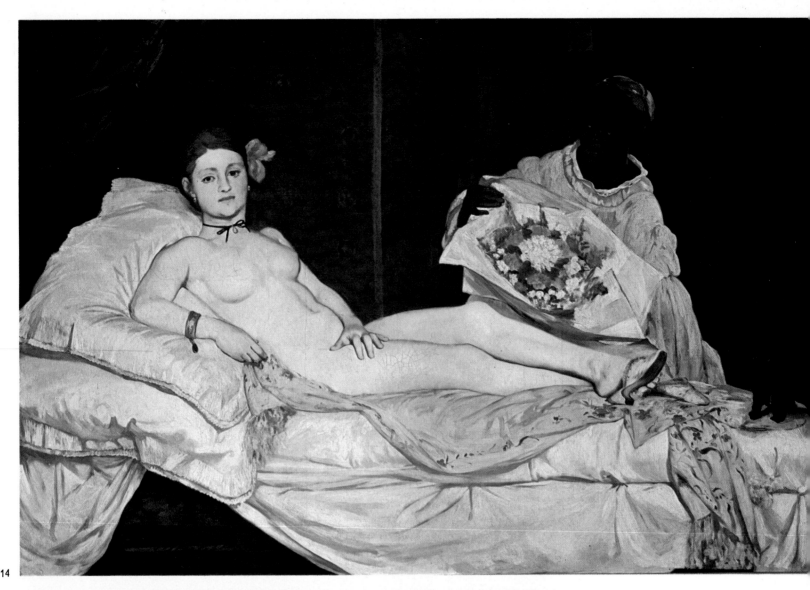

14

15

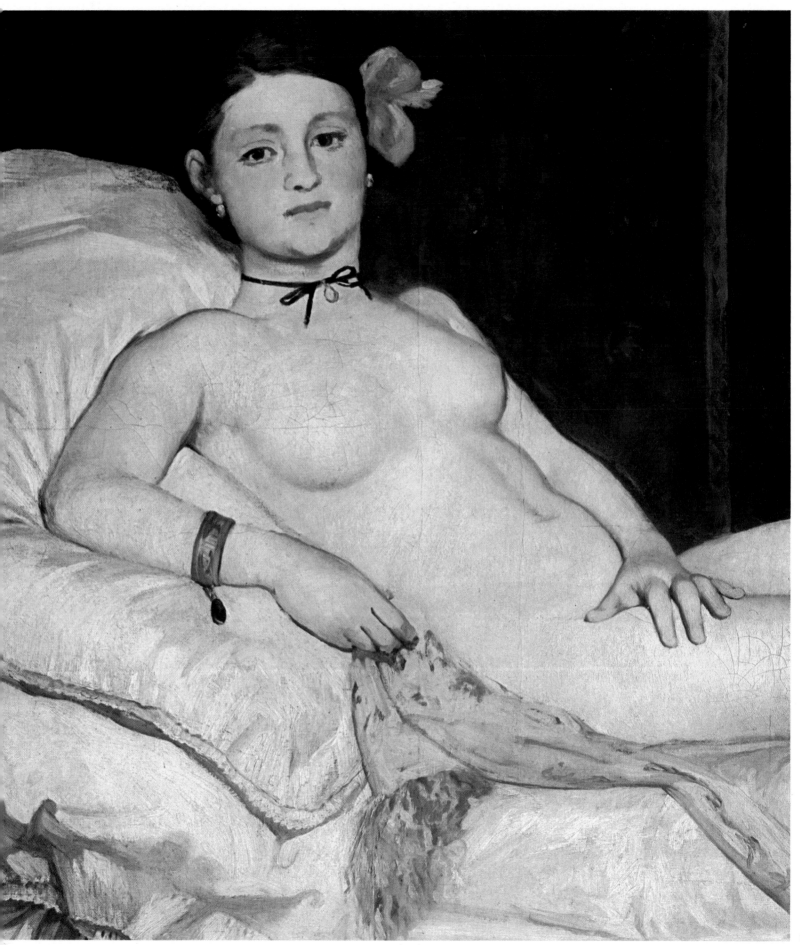

17

24

39

40

43

44

49